Introducing
the
German Idealists

Introducing
the
German Idealists

Mock Interviews with
KANT, HEGEL,
Fichte, Schelling, Reinhold,
Jacobi, Schlegel
and a letter from
SCHOPENHAUER

Robert C. Solomon

HACKETT PUBLISHING COMPANY
Indianapolis • Cambridge

Printed in the United States of America
First printing

For further information, please address
Hackett Publishing Company, Inc.
Box 55573, Indianapolis, Indiana 46205

Library of Congress Cataloging in Publication Data

Solomon, Robert C.
    Introducing the German idealists.

    Bibliography: p.
    1. Idealism. 2. Philosophy, German—19th
century. 3. Philosophy, German—18th century.
I. Title.
B2745.S67   141   81–891
ISBN 0-915145-02-2   AACR2
ISBN 0-915145-03-0 (pbk.)

My special thanks to Joe and Betty Hanson,
    to Kris,
    and to the students who prove to me
    every year that the most ponderous
    philosophers can still be fun
    to talk about.

Contents

PREFACE

Against the backdrop of the French Revolution and the Napoleonic conquest of Europe, the philosophers of Germany created the most ambitious and imaginative systems of thought of modern times. Most philosophy students today, however, never get to know them.

A few years ago the reason for their neglect was that most of these figures, with the exception of Immanuel Kant, were considered too disreputable, which is to say, out of fashion. Today, the problem is that all of them, including Kant, are considered too difficult. Most instructors, accordingly, skip the period altogether, alluding to Kant's great importance by giving the impression that between Kant and Bertrand Russell or Edmund Husserl at the beginning of the present century, the history of modern philosophy suffered an eclipse of sorts. (If a student takes an "existentialism" course, Kierkegaard and Nietzsche appear to be voices in the wilderness. And then, of course, there are Marx and Mill.)

This is an intellectual tragedy. The history of modern philosophy is wholly incomplete without some insight into the actual ideas of such giants as Kant and Hegel. But to tackle even one of their shorter works in an undergraduate class is almost always an act of pedagogical folly.

The same problem emerges regarding students of comparative and German literature, students of history and, especially, the history of ideas. There is not a reader who does not come across the names Kant, Fichte, Schelling and Hegel with impressive frequency in the context of the great poets and political movements, for example. But again, the vague references to their ideas are woefully brief and obscure, for any attempt to get a fair overview of their philosophies would require years of tedious study which most students—and their professors—are not willing to undertake (understandably, in most cases).

In this brief work, I present an extremely simplified survey of the major and minor figures who make up the philosophical mainstream in Germany around the turn and the early years of the nineteenth century. My intention is not to provide a substitute for serious study nor a complete textbook for a course in what has come to be called "German Idealism." There is no shortcut to scholarship, no replacing original texts. But it is my view that even a caricature drawn in fun, so long as it is sensitive to the character of the original, is far better for most readers than nothing at all—which seems to be the prevalent alternative.

Thus, while creating what I hope are amiable and reasonably accurate portraits, in the mock-interviews that follow, I have taken

1

some liberties and indulged in occasional frivolities. For, truth be told, these supposedly oh-so-somber personalities were, for the most part, embattled egomaniacs as well as self-conscious geniuses; and in their mutual hostility and competition, their views of each other were less than generous and their behavior not at all courteous. I have tried to portray these human and personal qualities of their philosophies as well as the more conceptual structures of their various systems, and I have unabashedly Americanized their nineteenth-century German manners and speech to make them more familiar to us. I hope that my importation of television into a period when this modern medium was undreamed of will not seem too outrageous, and that my irreverence will not be taken for disrespect. For geniuses or not, the German philosophers were first of all *characters,* and that is what makes them comprehensible.

The book falls into three parts; first, an interview with the un-disputed genius and founder of modern German philosophy, Immanuel Kant. I have set the interview in April 1790 when all of his main works, most recently his *Critique of Judgment,* had been published.

Second, to show the variety of interpretations and subsequent directions of argument that the Kantian enterprise inspired, I have arranged a symposium in memory of Kant (February 1804) with six of the major figures of post-Kantian philosophy. Few of them ever became well-known to English-speaking audiences, but they all had considerable influence in German literature and philosophy for years to come.

Of the six symposiasts, however, only one would emerge as a giant, whose status would be said by some to rival Kant. That was G. W. F. Hegel, who was virtually unknown at the time of Kant's death, but who by 1820 was indisputably the most powerful philosophical figure in Germany, perhaps in the world. The third part of the book, accordingly, is a personal interview with Hegel.

Finally, I have included a letter, completely made up but wholly in the temperament of Arthur Schopenhauer, who was among the most self-consciously faithful followers of Kant but who did not become well known for another half-century. He published *World as Will and Representation* in 1819, just when Hegel was reaching his apotheosis; his letter makes clear his reactions to Hegel's success.

I owe a debt of gratitude to Joshua Cohen of M.I.T. and Trudy R. Govier of Trent University for their reading of the first draft of this book and their helpful suggestions.

INTRODUCTION

"German Idealism" from Kant to Hegel

Philosophies are not created in an intellectual vacuum. Ideas, like fashions and inflation, are an integral aspect of society as a whole, a reaction to current events, an expression of the hopes and fears of the age. Philosophy is the abstract articulation of "the spirit of the times" (or *Zeitgeist*), and as formidable as the philosophical "systems" of Kant and his followers may appear to be, they are first of all expressions of and attempts to come to terms with very real and tangible questions about the world, about our place in the order of things, about the credibility of religious belief, about the desire to be "a good human being" and our concern for the quality of life in an increasingly hostile and impersonal world.

To understand the world of the German philosophers, we have to look beyond philosophy, for example, to the poets of Germany who were often their friends (Friedrich Hölderlin, for example, was Hegel's best friend in college, and the great poet Goethe had regular correspondence with Schelling). It may be necessary to familiarize ourselves with the then new economic theories of Adam Smith and Ricardo, just reaching Germany from England; these influenced Schiller and then the Idealists and, a half-century later, the young Karl Marx. We have to look at the battles within and about science in Germany, between the mechanics of Newtonian physics and the organic theories of Leibniz and Goethe, between the empirical methods of knowledge and the less rational feelings of faith and religion, particularly in Lutheran Germany. We would have to study the demographic shifts in population, the move to the cities, the growth of the "middle class," the newly awakened spirit of German nationalism and the international conflicts of the times. And in particular, of course, one has to look to the traumatic impact of the French Revolution and its violent aftermath, to the rise of "liberation movements" throughout Europe under Napoleon and the sudden shift in the politics of the world. The great systems of philosophy express and reflect these dramatic forces and influences, and many of their most difficult concepts can best be understood as abstract attempts to come to grips with them.

Most significant for an understanding of the German philosophers, however, are two cultural quasi-philosophical movements that were simultaneously achieving widespread recognition in Germany at the end of the eighteenth century. The first was a movement called *"The Enlightenment,"* which had a twin birth in England and France and its first dramatic realization in America.

(Thomas Jefferson and Benjamin Franklin, for example, both considered themselves part of the Enlightenment.) The Enlightenment placed strong emphases on the powers of human reason and the importance of science and philosophical criticism; on the universal equality and the rights of men; on the absolute supremacy of *humanity* over nature, the primacy of people before religion; and on the right of all people to participate in and indeed even to create their own forms of life and government. Immanuel Kant saw himself throughout his career as an explicit defender of the Enlightenment in Germany (called *"Aufklärung"*) and Fichte, Schelling, Hegel and the others were all influenced, both positively and negatively, by its basic claims and principles.

The second movement, which is often considered to be a reaction against the Enlightenment, is *Romanticism*. The German philosophers made a deep impression on the Romantics of the nineteenth century, but they were also influenced by self-styled Romantics of their own age and by an earlier generation of much-mentioned but now rarely read poets who called themselves *"Sturm und Drang"* ("storm and stress"). Against the Enlightenment, which stressed cosmopolitan internationalism and tended to treat German language and culture as inferior and "provincial," the Romantics placed their emphasis on local German customs and the intricacies of their own language. Thus, it is with pride that Goethe "teaches poetry to speak in German," and Hegel boasts that he will teach philosophy to speak German too. (In fact, of course, Kant had already done that.) In league with these poets was a one-time student of Kant who had turned into the arch-enemy of Enlightenment thinking, Johann Herder (1744-1803). He advocated the uniqueness of the German people (*"Volk"*) and the importance of customs and more "spiritual" values against the Enlightenment ideals of internationalism and universal Reason. Like the poets, he rejected the celebration of science as the highest achievement of the human mind and turned instead to poetry and peasant "superstitions," the anathema of "enlightened" thinkers. And with the great philosopher Leibniz (1646-1716) he attacked Newtonian physics for its mechanical view of nature and argued instead the more vital view of the universe as a living, developing organism, obeying its own inner principles rather than the laws of motion proposed by Isaac Newton. The Romantics preferred faith and mystery to Reason and knowledge; they sometimes tended to be extreme anti-intellectuals (in a very articulate and intellectual way, of course). They saw the Enlightenment as a *foreign* influence and preferred to develop views of their own.

All of this becomes extremely complex, however, in view of the fact that Enlightenment and Romanticism were never clearly distinguished in Germany. Leibniz, who was internationally recognized as a great scientist and mathematician, the intellectual equal of Newton and the great defender of Reason and internationalism, was also the source of the most vehement attacks on Newton's physics, insisting that the universe must be seen as living and developing rather than as a machine obeying mechanical laws. And it was Kant, the spokesman for the Enlightenment, who became the single most powerful influence on the philosophers who turned against the Enlightenment, and who himself, despite his enormous admiration for Newton, continued to accept the organic and often intentionally mysterious view of the universe as a living thing. Indeed, it is this view of the universe and of the human mind, too, with its emphasis on development according to internal principles rather than by the eternal mechanical laws of science, that will provide the core of German Idealism, even in the philosophy of Kant.

The emphasis on "inner" activity and evolution is the heart of German Idealism. "Idealism," simply defined, is the view that the world depends on ideas, that objects exist only insofar as they are objects of consciousness. Idealism denies the independent or "objective" existence of the physical world and insists instead that the world is, in some sense, a product of our own conscious activity. The word "activity" is crucial here, for there are forms of idealism, some of which were popular in England about the same time, which also insist that the world depends on "ideas" but give no particular role to our own conscious activity in the production of the world. Of course, what one means by "production" is the crucial question for idealists, and how one interprets the apparent "objectivity" of the world thus produced was the issue that, more than any other, would have the German idealists fighting among themselves. The most extreme idealists rejected the "objectivity" of the world altogether; others, Kant, for one, made it a function of conscious subjectivity.

For the American reader, who is accustomed to the more "common sense" tradition of the English enlightenment and our own more "nuts and bolts" thinking, German Idealism embodies at least two general demands which we find all but incomprehensible. The first is the demand for a philosophical "system" that seems to us to have no connection with our everyday experience but, at best, represents some conceptual fairy tale that might be understood as a metaphor about human life, knowledge, religion and morals. No matter how impressed one may be, for example, by the Hegelian image of a world-spirit sweeping through history and using entire nations as steps to its own self-realization, there is no easy way in which to apply this image to specific moral questions about what we ought to do, or of using the Hegelian philosophy to decide between competing scientific theories or religious doctrines. But this is wrongly interpreted by unsympathetic critics to mean that German Idealism consists *wholly* of metaphors, without significance for science or everyday moral and practical concerns.

Second, there is the almost obsessive emphasis on "self" and "subjectivity" in German philosophy, which prompted the American philosopher George Santayana to write a remarkably unsympathetic book titled *The Ego in German Philosophy;* his indictment was, of course, that the German philosophers were all egomaniacs. But this philosophical egomania has its perfectly innocent beginnings in the French philosopher Descartes' insistence that everything we know about the world is first of all a "thought" in our minds. Once one accepts that plausible suggestion, however qualified, it is an easy step to the view that nothing can be known except through consciousness, and a few more steps to the dilemma that either the world outside of consciousness is unknown and unknowable or the world itself is dependent on our consciousness of it. Given the alternatives, Idealism becomes the more plausible choice; and the view that in some sense the world depends on *me* begins to look like the inevitable conclusion—as well as the starting point—of philosophy.

German Idealism begins by taking for granted the Cartesian starting point that our knowledge of the world begins with our consciousness of it and tries to work out the consequences of this innocent supposition with a thoroughness that we might find absurd. Indeed, one might well take the Idealists' conclusions to be reductions to absurdity of the Cartesian viewpoint, and so reject that viewpoint and its simple starting point once and forever. But one generation's absurdity is another's obvious assumption, and to understand the German Idealists we must begin by sympathizing with what they took to be self-evident—that all knowledge of the world itself begins with human consciousness. Then we can watch with fascination to see where they go from there.

In Descartes' time, a person could say, 'I think, therefore I am.' In our age anybody who thinks can only conclude that he is not, unless masses of people can see him on television and tell him, yes, he is, too. In our age, Descartes would have said, 'I am televised, therefore I am.'

—Russell Baker, August 1980

With these words of wit in mind, I herein present Kant, Hegel and some of the leading German philosophers of the nineteenth century in their television debut.

—R.C.S.

Two things have always filled me with ever new and increasing admiration and awe: the starry heavens above and the moral law within.

Kant (Critique of Practical Reason)

Part I Immanuel Kant (22 April 1724—12 February 1804)

22 April 1790: A SPECIAL REPORT:

Good evening. This is Barbara Wahrheit for DBS news, on special assignment here in Königsberg. For those of you who don't know where Königsberg is, let me tell you that it is as far away from the heart of Europe as Minsk, and just as cold. It's situated at the far east end of East Prussia, tucked away on the Gulf of Danzig. And yet, here in Königsberg, five hundred miles from Berlin, we are going to meet the man who is now considered in Germany to be the greatest philosopher since Plato and Aristotle. His name is Immanuel Kant.

We have arrived just in time to celebrate the publication of the third and last of a series of books that Professor Kant calls *"Critiques."* In 1781 he published the *Critique of Pure Reason,* which set the philosophical world in awe of him. In 1788 he published the second *"Critique,"* the *Critique of Practical Reason;* and just last week, the third *"Critique,"* the *Critique of Judgment* appeared, which completes the trilogy. I have also been told that today is Professor Kant's sixty-sixth birthday, so this is indeed a day for celebration. Professor Kant has never been married, by the way; he lives by himself, very simply, near the University of Königsberg, where he has been teaching for almost forty-five years. Allegedly, he has never been out of Königsberg, even to visit, although he has been invited to speak and to teach at almost every major university in Europe.

It is almost time to begin the interview, and although Professor Kant is not yet here, I've been told that he has never been late for an appointment in his life. And, yes, here he is, quietly walking through the crowd which has gathered around the door of the seminar-room, obviously enjoying the lavish attention and smiling courteously to the dozens of people who have come to greet him. He is a slight figure of a man, quite properly dressed. Now he has reached the head of the seminar table and I can see that he is smiling at the gift of Madeira wine bought for him by his students. The room has suddenly become utterly silent. With a quick nod and an authoritative gesture, he thanks his audience and bids them to resume their conversations. The Professor is sitting down to chat with one of his colleagues, and we will join him shortly in the front of the room. Meanwhile, we will pause for station identification, and then we'll be right back with Professor Immanuel Kant, author of *The Critique of Judgment* and the philosopher who has been called the most brilliant thinker of modern times. This is Bar-

9

bara Wahrheit reporting to you live from Königsberg, East Prussia.

*   *   *

BW: Good evening, Professor Kant.

KANT: Good evening.

BW: Professor, your name is often mentioned in American philosophy classes, but no one seems to know much about your very important work.

KANT: I welcome the opportunity to correct that situation. I have nothing but enthusiastic expectations for America in the future. One of our poets, Johann Goethe—whom you may know—said it well:

> America, thou hast it better,
> Than our World, the Old One.

BW: How do you explain your great popularity here in Germany?

KANT: Well, I must admit that I have never worked for what you Americans would call "success." I am a philosopher, and I am concerned with ideas and rigorous thinking, not popular acclaim. Indeed, I do not think most people are capable of the rigorous thinking that philosophy requires, and I look at my popularity with distrust and, politically, with some anxiety.

BW: But I am impressed by the fact that so many people seem to admire and respect your work. In America, I suspect most people could not even *name* a living American philosopher, but here in Germany you seem to be a national institution.

KANT: I'm skeptical about how many people have actually read my works, rather than picked up some half-baked notion of my ideas in casual conversation. Our Prussian idiom is a bit more ponderous than you Americans will tolerate, and my writing is not always easy. But if you actually read my works, I think you'll find that the language is not all that difficult. I even write for some popular magazines.

BW: *Philosophy* in popular magazines?

KANT: Even in the newspapers. You have to remember that we Germans have always had a healthy respect for the importance of *ideas*. You Americans seem to think that philosophy and ideas in general are just theoretical abstractions, matters to argue about but not to let seriously influence the way in which you live. It's strange isn't it, considering you are the one nation on earth that has actually been built out of ideas. They are European ideas, of course, but you've done so well with them. Your recent constitution for example.

BW: We appreciate your compliment, Professor, but do you really think philosophy itself can make a difference?

KANT: Look at this upheaval that has just taken place in France. As you probably know, I and many of my compatriots have been following the events in France with enormous interest and enthusiasm, and the reason is simple. That is no local disruption; it is not a temporary reaction of people who have suffered a hard winter and are overtaxed; it is a revolution of *ideas*—born of ideas, motivated by ideas, and it will be driven to its conclusion by ideas. In fact, I daresay the ideas that underlie the events in France are just the same ideas that are embodied in my own philosophy.

BW: Would you say that you are a revolutionary philosopher, then?

KANT: Yes. In fact, I call my own philosophy a "Copernican Revolution," literally turning our old view of the world around, questioning the standpoint that is never questioned. But the upheaval in France, strictly speaking, is not a "revolution." The King gave the power to the Assembly and now they are using it.

BW: Did you follow our American revolution a few years ago?

KANT: Yes, but that was not a revolution but simply a war for independence.

BW: Do you approve?

KANT: Yes, it was marvelous, simply marvelous! Of course you had a much easier time of it than the French; you only had to throw out an irritating and in any case somewhat distracted foreign sovereign, some three thousand miles away; you didn't have to rebuild society from the ground up. But I wholly approve of your principles: the demand for your own autonomy, your own moral and political freedom to use your own independent reason.

BW: You don't find the French uprisings ominous?

KANT: "Ominous"? No, no; you Americans do tend to be conservative. And these are no mere "uprisings." I have no doubt that there will be some bloody years ahead, for what they are attempting to do is indeed quite difficult. I expect the King will be indecisive and unsure of what to do with the new demands, and I expect that the demands themselves will get more and more extreme until, finally, the people will demand what they really want, a government of their own, a government by the general will, as their greatest philosopher, Jean-Jacques Rousseau, has told them. There's this lawyer chap Robespierre, for example—a man of my own heart. I've been reading some of his newspaper articles. He's a fellow to watch.

BW: I am surprised to hear you so enthusiastic about the revolution; frankly, I would have expected that you would be far more reserved.

KANT: It's not a cause for reservation, but for exhilaration.

BW: Do you envision a similar revolution here in Prussia?

KANT: No, no, no, no. [*slight pause*] No, no.

BW: I don't understand; surely you don't think the government of Frederick Wilhelm is any better than the reign of Louis XVI in France, and surely . . .

KANT: [*nervously*] Each nation has its own contribution to make to the world; the French have their politics, we Germans intend to revolutionize the world of the spirit. And personally, I abhor change. [*abruptly*] Now you asked me, if I'm not mistaken, why my philosophy is so popular, and I answered "because we Germans take our ideas very seriously." But there is more to it than that.

BW: Yes?

KANT: [*relieved*] Yes; you may think that philosophy is an esoteric discipline practiced by a bunch of old men sitting around wondering whether the world exists and inventing some exotic language in which to disguise their nonsense, but that isn't it at all.

BW: I never . . .

KANT: Philosophy is concerned with nothing less than the ruling ideas of human life—what we can know, what we should believe, what we ought to do, what we can hope. I may write as if I am answering other intellectuals, people such as David Hume and our own great Leibniz,[1] but I am really writing for the common man, about our common concerns.

---

1. Gottfried Wilhelm von Leibniz (1646-1716), scientist, mathematician, diplomat, philosopher, "the last of the universal geniuses." He invented the calculus before Newton and invented one of the first computers. Kant himself was a disciple of Christian Wolff, who was a disciple of Leibniz, so Leibniz' philosophy, even if rarely mentioned, plays an enormous role in the philosophy of German Idealism.

David Hume (1711-1776) was a Scottish philosopher who would also play a decisive role in Kant's philosophizing; both philosophers will be mentioned frequently throughout the interview.

BW: You know, a German philosopher named Nietzsche, writing almost a century from now, will say that your joke on posterity is to defend the common man in terms that the common man can not possibly understand.

KANT: Ha ha. Really? I guess that is true; nevertheless, that is what I am defending—our instinctive sense of curiosity and wonder, our distinctly human ability to reason, to reflect on principles and choose among them—the starry skies above, the moral law within—that is what continually intrigues me, and fascinates us all.

BW: Why does that need defending?

KANT: It does, assuredly. If you look at what is happening in Europe today, and in America too, I don't think you can even question my claim that everything is in turmoil; the world is being turned upside down. Authorities who have been unquestioned for a thousand years have suddenly been called to account for themselves, and they are ridiculed and discredited. Once we believed what the pope told us to believe; we believed without question that the interests of the king were the interests of the nation; once we believed that the earth stood still and was circled by the sun. But now we have turned against authority; we have determined it is up to *us* to decide what is believable. And it is no surprise that in the midst of the turmoil, faced with this responsibility, some people have argued that *nothing* is believable—except, perhaps, one's own selfish interests and the immediate experiences of the senses. And others are insisting on an unprecedented wave of repression and censorship. Now that, you must admit, is indeed a crisis!

BW: Yes, I certainly will admit that. How does your philosophy resolve that crisis?

KANT: I am concerned, as are all philosophers, to show what can be believed and what cannot, to prove the first and refute the latter. The word *"Critique"* that appears in my titles is just what it means: to criticize, to evaluate what we believe and why we believe it, to see what we can know and what we can't.

BW: But when you begin questioning everything, will there be anything left?

KANT: Of course. Being critical doesn't mean rejecting everything. When Martin Luther rejected the infallibility of the pope and turned instead to the dictates of his own conscience, he did not give up the faith; he did not abandon his belief in God; rather, he found the source of his faith and its laws *in himself*. He didn't change religions so much as he changed religion's *grounds*. So too, although a person may decide that merely because some prohibition is a law of the state is not a sufficient reason to obey it, it doesn't mean that he goes out and ignores all laws and indulges in killing, stealing and fornicating; there are other reasons for prohibitions besides the fact that they're laws of the state. The problem of philosophy is to find the *right* reasons.

BW: So what your "critique" is about is trying to justify what the common man believes, through philosophy?

KANT: Yes. I want to defend our confidence in ourselves, to know the world and know the truth. I think it is a scandal, for example, that no one has refuted Hume's skeptical doubts about the existence of "the external world" which he published a half-century ago. And I want to defend the morals that we all learned at our mothers' knees, and the religious faith we learned there, too.

BW: Do you believe in God, Professor?

KANT: Yes, without qualification. Don't believe some of those histrionics in the conservative press accusing me of undermining everything good, true and sacred. I have only reestablished traditional values on new and firmer ground, since the old grounds have been eaten away and are ready to cave in. You see, I am a revolutionary in my thinking, but I am conservative in my conclusions, as well as in my personal life: I still believe in God, country, morals and human knowledge.

BW: You are a scientist too, aren't you Professor? I understand you've published papers in physics and astronomy.

KANT: Yes, that is the source of my concern for knowledge and of my immense admiration for Isaac Newton. But it is not just science that is important, it is reason in general. My philosophy, and the Enlightenment as a whole, is a program to give people confidence in their own mental abilities, to put an end to superstition and that peculiar human frailty that leads people to turn to authority for the answers instead of trusting themselves.

BW: A few years ago you wrote an essay called "What is Enlightenment?" and your answer sounds very much like what you are saying now. You do consider yourself a part of that international movement, don't you?

KANT: Yes, I am very much a part of it. We call it the "Aufklärung" here in Germany, and I am very proud to be in league with such great and enlightened human beings as Voltaire, Rousseau, John Locke, David Hume, and your own Thomas Jefferson.

BW: In your essay, you defined "enlightenment" as simply "dare to know!" Is that how you would still define the movement?

KANT: Yes; it is just what we've been talking about, really: a sense of finding out for oneself, a sense that the truth will make you free.

BW: But isn't the Enlightenment an atheistic movement, based on Isaac Newton's conclusions that the universe is nothing but a giant machine, governed by the laws of gravity and motion, with no room for human freedom or consciousness or God?

KANT: There are some French philosophers who have argued something like that[2] but that is not the Enlightenment itself. Even Voltaire believed in God; and in my philosophy, at any rate, there can be no question but that I do believe in human freedom, and consciousness, and God. And in Newton's discoveries, as well. But it's important for you to note that Newton did not have that view of the universe which you ascribe to him; he believed devoutly in God and spent most of his life trying to put his physics and his theology together.

BW: Really? The picture we always get is of a "Godless universe," "mere matter in motion," and nothing else.

KANT: Not at all. I do agree with Newton that knowledge requires an understanding of the phenomena of nature, but I also think—and he did too—that much more than that is required for a rational vision of the universe.

BW: In one of your books you wrote, "I have limited knowledge to make room for faith." Is that what you mean?

KANT: Yes. My whole system of philosophy is based on the idea that Newton's physics and its principles are absolutely necessary for our understanding of the world, but that a totally different conception is required by reason, in order to live a good life. You can't claim a serious belief in God if you view the world merely as a giant watch, even if you acknowledge that some power had to make the watch and wind it. I do not believe that man can live without God. Similarly, you can't believe in human freedom and our responsibility for our actions if you think of people as robots, machines that blindly follow the cause-and-effect laws of nature. But it is impossible to think of oneself as a robot. So what I have in mind is to separate the two, to defend Newton on the one hand, and to defend freedom, morality and religion on the other.

BW: I'm sorry Professor, I'm not sure I understand; why can't you hold people responsible for their actions if you believe in cause-and-effect?

2. E.g., the Baron Paul Henri d'Holbach (1723–89) who did insist that nothing is real except matter in motion.

KANT: I didn't say that; of course one must believe in cause-and-effect, even in human actions. For example, I reach down to pick up this glass of Madeira so kindly provided for me, and of course there is a cause—my willing my arm to move—and an effect—my arm moving; there is another cause—my tilting the glass—and its effect—mmm, the wine going into my mouth. Thank you. Quite good!

BW: But why does cause-and-effect raise a problem about responsibility?

KANT: Because of the first step, the first cause. If you believe that my *will* was also caused by, let's say, my brain, by my Prussian upbringing, by my intense attachment to my mother, by the influences of the stars, then my action becomes just another event in a chain of causes and effects, none of which are in my control. To hold someone responsible for an action means that he or she could have done otherwise. I am responsible for drinking that wine because I could have decided not to; I could have decided not to will the glass to my lips. I could have poured it on the table. I could have politely said "no."

BW: So to hold someone responsible means that his will, the first step in deciding to do something, is not caused by anything.

KANT: There are influences on our behavior, of course, but the will cannot be determined. There must be freedom.

BW: And so you have to believe that people are free—that their wills are uncaused—in order to believe in moral responsibility.

KANT: Yes.

BW: Then there are exceptions to Newton's laws of nature?

KANT: No. But I will have to explain that later.

BW: Please do, Professor, but first, we must take time out for a minute and return to our local stations for station identification.

*   *   *

BW: Professor Kant, in the Preface of your first "critique," the *Critique of Pure Reason,* you say that your fundamental concern is the problem of *"metaphysics,"* which formerly was considered "the Queen of Sciences" but now is in ill repute. But that doesn't sound much like what we've been talking about, nor does it sound like a problem that ordinary people are worried about.

KANT: Oh, but it is! What I mean by "metaphysics" is that set of principles in which we all have to believe in order to live as rational human beings. I am not talking about the rather abstract systems of beliefs that philosophers have invented and go on arguing about among themselves, although they too are usually concerned with the same sets of concerns. Metaphysics ultimately comes down to three basic beliefs, which I simply summarize as "God, Freedom and Immortality." I do not believe that anyone can rationally consider the world and not believe in a Supreme Being. And I do not believe that anyone can be rationally moral and not believe in his or her own freedom, or, for that matter, in his or her own immortality, for it is only in the province of God that our virtue will surely be rewarded.

BW: That sounds more like Christianity than metaphysics to me, Professor.

KANT: It is Christianity, of course, but it is also metaphysics. Please don't think that metaphysics has to be obscure and irrelevant to everyday activity; metaphysics is the basis of human life.

BW: And is that all there is to metaphysics, "God, Freedom and Immortality"?

KANT: Well, no, not really. If you take the word "metaphysics" a bit more loosely it includes all sorts of basic principles, for example, the basic principles of knowledge, nature, morality, art.

BW: What do you mean by "basic principles"?

KANT: Those rules and assumptions without which one couldn't even begin to understand a realm of human endeavor. For example, a person couldn't comprehend even the simplest theory in science if he or she did not accept the validity of the idea of cause-and-effect, and one could hardly appreciate a work of art without the idea of beauty.

BW: But if metaphysics includes knowledge, nature, morality and art, then doesn't metaphysics include almost everything?

KANT: Yes and no. Every human endeavor has its metaphysical principles, that is, the rules and assumptions that define its foundations, but there is another sense of "metaphysics" that has been extremely powerful throughout the history of philosophy which I utterly reject, and that is the idea of metaphysics as knowledge of things as they are, apart from our experience of them, or what I call the "things-in-themselves."

BW: You don't believe in "things-in-themselves"?

KANT: That question is more complicated than you might think, but for the moment let me say that I do believe in things-in-themselves but I don't believe that we can know anything about them. May I ask you to permit me to explain my answer later in the interview?

BW: With pleasure. I promise to do so, Professor.

KANT: May I suggest, then, that we proceed to the business itself? So far we have only been skirting around my philosophy, like a timid tourist in a museum.

BW: All right, where should we start, Professor Kant?

KANT: At the beginning, of course.

BW: And where is that?

KANT: Well, we have already begun with the idea that my philosophy is about the age-old conflict between knowledge and faith, and I have tried to show how we can and must believe both in the modern picture of the physical universe and in the traditional wisdom of morality and the Christian religion, so I would think the place for us to begin now is to explain *how* I intend to defend my position.

BW: Let's start with knowledge.

KANT: Good, that's what my first *Critique* is about.

BW: Why does knowledge have to be defended?

KANT: Let me answer you by telling you something about my own experiences. I have been a philosopher for a long time. For many years I was a disciple of Christian Wolff, perhaps not a great philosopher himself but a clearheaded and faithful disciple of Gottfried Wilhelm Leibniz, the first truly great German philosopher. Leibniz was a metaphysician in the old sense, trying to tell us what the world "really" had to be like "in itself," behind the appearances of everyday life. He wove a fantastic picture of the universe, which I now find hard to accept, in which he envisioned the basic units of reality as self-enclosed minds—great numbers of them—which he called *monads.* None of the monads had any relationship to any other monads except to one *supermonad,* which was God. God programmed all the monads to have experiences *as if* they were in actual physical relationship with the other monads, which they were not. And God, in his mind, knew all these relations to be necessary.[3] I know it sounds a bit ridiculous in this simplified way of describing it, but you must believe me that it was utterly brilliant, and even the parts that sound the most preposterous are in fact very clever solutions to

3. Leibniz actually defended the more technical thesis that, for God, all true statements are "analytic," or logically true. And because in traditional logic all analytically true statements are logically equivalent, they can all be reduced to a single statement, which Leibniz summarizes as "$A = A$," or the "Law of Identity." This bit of jargon is important for us because the German Idealists often make use of this equation without even mentioning Leibniz or the logical context in which it gains its meaning.

extremely difficult philosophical questions. At any rate, I believed in much of this and I used to teach a kind of Leibnizian
system, in which I was confident in the powers of human reason
to validate some such knowledge of the way the world "really"
is, "in itself," when I came across a British philosopher named
David Hume . . . Ah, you know about Hume? Well it was
Hume, if I may use a phrase I have often used before, who
awakened me from my dogmatic slumbers. In other words, I had
simply assumed, without being critical at all, the Leibnizian view
that human reason is capable of knowing about the way the
world "really" is, apart from the way it seems to us, that is, "in
itself." What Hume argued was equally brilliant and utterly
devastating to my sure beliefs. Hume argued that all of our
knowledge comes to us through our senses—an old empiricist
thesis he learned from the London physician John Locke.[4] It
sounds like an innocent idea but—and this is an enormous
"but"—it had profound consequences. Hume showed that
human reason could not, on this basis, come to actually know
anything about the world independent of an individual's experiences of it. Indeed, he claimed that we could not even know
that there was a world independent of our experiences. He
showed that such basic beliefs as our daily confidence that the
sun will rise tomorrow, or that water comes to a boil, rather than
freezes, when sufficiently heated, could not be defended by appeal to experience, nor to reason either. The upshot of the argument was that we cannot really know anything, that reason is im-
potent when it comes to justifying even the most obvious principles of human knowledge—such as "there is a world out there"
or "every event is caused by other events." And because Hume
was also a member in good standing of the Enlightenment, his
conclusions were particularly upsetting to me, for he used the
Enlightenment ideal of reason against itself, to show by some
brilliant reasoning that reason couldn't really prove anything.

BW: But Hume didn't really believe that we didn't know anything, did he?

KANT: No, of course not; he said that what he believed he believed according to the wisdom of "nature," and nature took
care of what reason could not do. In fact, he argued, we can't
help believing as we do, as matters of instinct, habit or custom.

BW: Isn't that sufficient?

KANT: No, it is not sufficient—indeed it is a scandal—because the
whole Enlightenment, the whole celebration of the powers of

---

4. John Locke (1632-1704), the first great "British empiricist" and the founder of
modern political liberalism.

human reason to tell what's true from what's false, what's right from what's wrong, to eliminate superstition (which is "natural" too) and to provide us with confidence in ourselves, turns on our confidence in reason. And Hume himself wasn't always consistent about how to apply his scepticism. He continued to accept Newton's physics—invalidly I would argue, as he presupposed the validity of Newton's causal theories in his own demonstration that we have no rational right to believe in causality—but with regard to theology he declared with arrogance: "Let's condemn it all to the flames, for it can contain nothing but sophistry and illusion." What if someone decided to say the same thing about Newton's physics and the whole of human knowledge, as in fact some of my German compatriots are doing right at this minute? Hume must be refuted. It was clear to me then, and it is clear to me now, that what I did was absolutely necessary. Not only the Enlightenment but our whole conception of ourselves was at stake. If we can't be certain of our ability to know, then once again we are like little children appealing blindly to authority, trying to understand reality but not trusting our own faculties to do so.

BW: So your first *Critique* is really the refutation of Hume's scepticism?

KANT: It is not just that, of course, but it is in part my answer to Hume. It is also my reworking of Leibniz, to whom I have had allegiance for some fifty years. And of Newton too, who is more than anyone my enduring intellectual hero.

BW: But it is Hume who seems to move you the most. You begin one section, "all knowledge begins with experience"; that sounds exactly like Hume's empiricism, doesn't it?

KANT: Ah, yes, but the second and just as important part of that sentence is "all knowledge does not arise *from* experience." Indeed, that phrase is the key to my whole philosophy, that we do not simply infer knowledge from experience, or from reason either, but rather, *we contribute* forms and principles to our experience.

BW: Is this the "Copernican revolution" you mentioned?

KANT: Yes, the "revolution" is the suggestion that our experience does not simply conform to objects "outside of us," but rather that objects must conform to the forms of our experience. We do not just passively learn about the world; we also contribute to the world; we "constitute" it as it is, as your Constitution "sets up" the forms of your government.

BW: Do you mean we actually *create* the world of our experience?

KANT: "Create"? No. No one—except perhaps God—can create an object, at least a physical object, just by thinking about it. When I insist that we actively contribute to our experience, I do not want anyone to think that we thereby just "make it up," which would be absurd. First of all, we don't have any choice about the raw materials of experience, our sensations, which I call the *"manifold of intuition."* Sensations are simply *given* to us; we passively receive them, and we have no choice in the matter.

BW: Do you mean that they are caused in us by objects? By the things-in-themselves?

KANT: Intelligent question, but let me delay my answer. The important point for now is that we don't have any choice in the matter. I am looking over there [*glances toward a large woman wearing a bright green sweater*] and I have an intuition of green, a perception I am unable to control; I'm not just making it up.

BW: That seems obvious enough.

KANT: The second constraint on our constitution of objects is the fact that our minds are structured so that only certain kinds of experience are possible. For example, space and time are structures of our minds, or more accurately, I call them *"a priori forms of intuition."* They are *forms* of intuition because, however we organize our experience into discrete objects, they must exist in three-dimensional space and one-dimensional time, and there can only be one such space, one such time. I call them *a priori* because these forms come *before* any particular experience; our experience conforms to the forms. We don't have any choice about it, and it would be simply stupid to say that we "choose" to experience the world in this way. There is, for us, no other way.

BW: By "for us" do you mean that the world might really "in itself" be some other way?

KANT: I can't answer that question, because I can't know anything about the way the world is—or might be—"in itself," apart from our experience of it. But I can say that God, who is not limited in His knowledge as we are, might see all of time at once and have experiences everywhere at once, and thus not see the world "in" space and time as we do.

BW: Are there other constraints? Besides the given *manifold of intuition* and the *a priori* form of space and time?

KANT: Yes, there are quite a few, and most of my philosophy is aimed at spelling them out. For example, another set of constraints on our constitution of experience are those *concepts* we use to organize them. Like the forms of space and time, these too are *a priori,* that is, contributed to our experience rather than simply read from our experience. The concept of a horse, for example, we learn *from* experience; but the concept of a physical object we do not ever learn—we supply that *to* our experience, even as infants. I call these a priori concepts *categories,* and you might say that the categories provide us with the rules according to which we must organize the world.

BW: Why "must"?

KANT: Because they are the only categories we have, the only categories we *can* have. This is what I prove in my *Critique.*

BW: "The only game in town."

KANT: [*dim smile*] Yes, as you say, "the only game in town."

BW: How did you determine your list of categories?

KANT: Our psychologists established the list; I have borrowed it from them.

BW: What are these categories?

KANT: Oh, you can guess the main ones; the category of *substance,* which means simply that the objects of knowledge must be viewed as having their own existence "outside" of us.

BW: You mean that we constitute objects in our minds according to the rule that we experience them as not in our minds?

KANT: Yes, that's just about it. Another category is *causality;* it is also part of my answer to Hume. He suggested that cause-and-effect relations were just associations in our minds; I answer him that cause-and-effect is a necessary rule according to which we *must* interpret all of our experiences.

BW: Why?

KANT: Because otherwise our intuitions would be chaos, with no sense of order, no possibility of understanding.

BW: So, again, we constitute it in our minds but have to experience it as if it were in the world?

KANT: No, be careful; it is not *as if* it were in the world; it *is* in the world. The world is, I am arguing, only what we make it.

BW: That is, given the manifold of intuition and according to the rules or categories that are necessary for us.

KANT: Yes, precisely; the world is as we constitute it.

BW: How does this refute Hume's scepticism? He said that we can't know anything but our experiences. Are you saying anything different from that?

KANT: Yes indeed, I am saying that the world *is* the world of our experiences.

BW: But what about the things-in-themselves?

KANT: Ah, yes, we'll get back to that.

BW: So your theory, your "Copernican revolution," is that the world necessarily conforms to our conceptions of it, instead of the old view, which culminated in Hume's scepticism, that we have to find out whether our concepts conform to the way the world "really" is, apart from our experience.

KANT: Yes, because then you can never know, for you can never experience anything outside of your experiences. On my view, the basic principles of knowledge—our belief in a world "outside" of us, our belief that every event in nature has its causes and an explanation—these are necessary and immune from scepticism just because we ourselves supply them, *must* supply them, to every possible experience.

You said, jokingly, that the categories "are the only game in town." Indeed, the principles of knowledge are unquestionable and irrefutable in the same way that the rules of chess are unquestionable and irrefutable while you're playing the game; you agree to the rules just by playing the game, and you can't change them without ceasing to play the game. So too, the forms of knowledge are *a priori* for us; to play the game of knowledge, to try to find out something true about the world, is to accept those rules: that the world is real, that causes are real, that every event has its causes and so on. And there is no alternative. Not to accept those rules, as some of our mystics in Königsberg do not, is to talk nonsense. For example, my late good friend and neighbor Johann Hamann[5] was like that; he refused to play the game of knowledge. He thought reality is something other than the rules of substance and causality, that you merely have to "feel it," not think about it. So I tried to tell him that he talked nonsense.

BW: But you still got along?

KANT: Oh, we did, marvelously. He thought I was a rationalist old fuddy-duddy. [*sentimental laugh*]

BW: [*restrained smile*] Thank you, Professor Kant. [*to camera*] We'll be back in a moment with more of the critical philosophy, but first, here is a word from your local sponsor.

*   *   *

BW: Professor Kant, you mentioned to me during the commercial break that you thought you should give the audience more of an overview of your work.

5. Johann Georg Hamann (1730–1788) was also a philosopher in Königsberg, who argued that true knowledge could be gained only through intuition, not rational

KANT: Yes, philosophy is nothing if not systematic, and I don't want your viewers to think that I'm merely providing potshots at Hume and a variety of opinions on an assortment of subjects.

BW: I'm sure they don't, Professor; I expect sales of the *Critique of Pure Reason* to reach the best-seller list after this broadcast. But please, explain your system to us.

KANT: Well, first of all, I have written three *Critiques,* as you know; the first one is concerned with knowledge; the second with practical matters—morality, mainly, but also religious belief. The third one, which I have just published, ties the first two together and also includes my theory of art.

BW: Is the strategy the same in all of them? Are they all part of the same "Copernican revolution?"

KANT: Yes, in each case I turn the traditional viewpoint around; people think that the truth is given to them through common sense, or the senses, whereas I argue that we actually *make* it true by the way in which we apply our principles to the world.

BW: And in the *Critique of Pure Reason* what you show is how we make the world of knowledge true by "constituting" it according to our own rules, or *categories?*

KANT: Yes. And that is how the *Critique of Pure Reason* is structured. Let me show you: [*the camera pans to a chart on the wall*]

THE CRITIQUE OF PURE REASON

faculty of the mind   *part of the Critique*

sensibility   *Transcendental Aesthetic*

understanding   *Transcendental Analytic*⎫
                                                      ⎬ *Transcendental Logic*
reason   *Transcendental Dialectic*⎭

---

thought. He rejected Kant's emphasis on science and preferred the unquestioning certitude of faith.

KANT: There are three faculties of the human mind.

BW: How do you know that?

KANT: [*slightly irritated*] I found that out from the psychologists. The three faculties are *sensibility, understanding* and *reason.* The first is passive and allows us to receive sensations through the apparatus of the senses (our eyes, ears, nose, tongue, skin and "inner sense"). It gives us the manifold of intuition. Both the faculties of understanding and reason are active, and both of them are concerned with the manipulation of concepts. Understanding applies concepts, and in particular the categories, to experience. Understanding and sensibility together are the faculties that give us *knowledge.* We come to know the world by applying the *a priori* concepts of the understanding, or categories, to the manifold of intuition.

BW: And what about reason?

KANT: Reason is also a faculty of concepts, but it does not apply concepts to experience. Reason is the faculty of *pure* concepts . . .

BW: Is that what you mean in your title by "Pure Reason"?

KANT: Yes, my concern is what reason alone can give us.

BW: What can it give us?

KANT: Logic, for example; that is one simple example of the manipulation of concepts without applying them to experience.

BW: And mathematics?

KANT: Ah, good; you might think so. Indeed, most philosophers —including Hume and Leibniz, for example—have thought so. But no, mathematics, and geometry too, are not a matter of pure reason. I'll explain why in a minute.

BW: What else does reason do, then?

KANT: Perhaps it is more important to say what it *cannot* do; it cannot give us knowledge of objects—in particular, knowledge of things as they are in themselves.

BW: But isn't the whole history of philosophy, that is, at least the history of metaphysics, the story of philosophers trying to use reason to figure out what the world is like "in itself"?

KANT: That's right.

BW: So in fact you are rejecting the whole history of metaphysics!

KANT: Most of it, at any rate. It is only by rejecting this part of metaphysics that we can avoid skepticism, for if you believe in the existence of a world beyond experience it is difficult to see how we could ever come to know that world. But now let me explain my *Critique*. It's rather elegant, actually.

The first part of the book is concerned with the *a priori* forms of sensibility or intuition, namely, space and time. I call it the *"Transcendental Aesthetic."* The word "aesthetic," which in some circles has come to mean "art," simply means "feeling," and it includes everything having to do with the senses.[6] The word "transcendental," which is one of the most important terms of my philosophy, refers to the necessary conditions of all experience. The "transcendental aesthetic," therefore, is my demonstration of the basic and necessary forms of experience, which are space and time.

Now I can answer your earlier question too, although not in any detail. Mathematics and geometry are not functions of pure reason but the formal articulation of the *a priori* forms of intuition; arithmetic is the articulation of our sense of time; more obviously, geometry is the articulation of the way in which we must perceive space. Ever since the Greeks, scientists have wondered how it is that an abstract number system can apply so well to our experiences of the world, whereas a merely formal system of symbols cannot. I have an answer for them: arithmetic is necessarily faithful to the world because the world is formed out of the same forms that we capture in our arithmetic. And geometers ever since Plato have wondered why it is that Euclidean geometry, which looks like an arbitrary list of definitions and axioms, nevertheless provides what seems to be the *only* set of theorems that describes the world of our experience. I now have an answer for them too.

BW: That's very exciting! So this means that mathematics and geometry are, really, descriptions of the structure of the human mind?

KANT: Something like that, but notice, too, that my "transcendental aesthetic" is my way of reconciling Leibniz and Newton, my two heroes.

BW: How is that? How did they disagree?

KANT: Newton assumed that space and time were "absolute"—that they exist "in themselves"; that space would still be space and time would still be time even if the universe were entirely empty, if there were no distances or durations to measure and, in any case, no standard of measurement either. Now you know that I think highly of the world of Newton's physics, but I could never buy the idea of an empty universe. I always agreed with Leibniz that space and time are dependent on relationships

6. The word was first used to refer to artistic feeling, rather than feeling in general, just about the time Kant was writing, in the late eighteenth century.

between things, not least importantly, relationships with the observer. But unfortunately Leibniz added to his theory the absurd view that space and time are *nothing but* relationships in the mind, and not outside of us at all. I have invented a compromise; space and time are "in us" insofar as they are the forms of our intuition, but they are thereby the forms of the world outside of us. We can imagine an empty universe only because it isn't really empty; we are still in it, doing the imagining, and we think that, because we can think of some empty finite space—which is easy—we can imagine an empty infinite universe as such.

BW: But space and time are relative to our consciousness of them?

KANT: Yes.

BW: Let me ask you about the second part of your book, which I see you call the *"transcendental logic."*

KANT: Yes. My transcendental logic has two parts, a *"transcendental analytic"* and a *"transcendental dialectic."* As you can guess, the analytic is about the *a priori* concepts of the understanding, and the dialectic is . . .

BW: About the *a priori* forms of reason.

KANT: No! You mustn't anticipate me unless you've been paying complete attention; I said that I wanted to do a "critique" of pure reason, and show what reason *cannot* do, namely, to know things-in-themselves. The "transcendental dialectic" is rather a demonstration of the *illusions* of metaphysical thinking.

BW: So the three parts aren't exactly parallel.

KANT: No; the transcendental aesthetic and the transcendental analytic demonstrate the *a priori* forms and concepts of experience, whereas the transcendental dialectic is concerned with the *limits of knowledge.*

BW: The strategy in the first two parts is to show that these forms and concepts *must* be of a certain sort.

KANT: Yes, I call my arguments *"transcendental arguments,"* accordingly. They justify a concept or a principle by showing that it is a necessary condition of experience. They show us what our experience *must* be like.

BW: What about the "transcendental dialectic"?

KANT: It is more complicated. Perhaps all I should do here for you is list its negative conclusions: first of all, I conclude that there can be no knowledge of things-in-themselves outside of our experience. At most, we might suppose that there must *be* some such things, but only as theoretical constructs, about which we can know nothing at all. "X–the unknown" I sometimes call the thing-in-itself.

BW: Sounds like a horror story.

KANT: Considering the way in which some philosophers have misunderstood me, it is.

BW: So you don't believe in the things-in-themselves?

KANT: I didn't say that; I said we couldn't have *knowledge* of them.

BW: Please continue.

KANT: Second, I argue that there can be no knowledge of the human soul, that the soul cannot be a thing of any kind.

BW: But . . .

KANT: Third, I argue that we cannot ever prove that God exists; we cannot know God and we cannot know, for example, that He created the world or that He is all-knowing or all-powerful.

BW: But . . .

KANT: Yes?

BW: But didn't you begin by telling us that two of the most important and necessary beliefs we have are belief in the immortality of the human soul and our belief in a supreme being?

KANT: Ah yes, but I did not say *knowledge* of them.

BW: Oh.

KANT: And finally, I show a rather dramatic consequence of pure Reason, namely, that it traps us in inescapable contradictions, which I call *antinomies.*

BW: What is an "antinomy"?

KANT: Briefly, it is a contradiction between two seemingly sound and equally valid principles. For example, philosophers and scientists have argued for centuries whether the universe has a beginning in time or whether it has been going on forever. I show that because there is no evidence that can prove one argument or the other, reason alone can prove *both* positions to be absolutely right on the basis of perfectly sound and valid arguments.

BW: You mean both views are true?

KANT: No, of course not. They're contradictory; one says there was a beginning, the other says that there was not. They can't both be true. What this means is that arguments from pure reason are unsound and must be rejected even when they seem to be perfectly valid.

BW: So you reject reason altogether then?

KANT: No, I reject reason as a method of gaining knowledge about the world. It has other functions which, as soon as I finish this glass of wine, I will be happy to discuss with you.

BW: Let's return to our local stations, then, for a brief commercial or two.

*   *   *

BW: Professor Kant, you promised to tell us about the other functions of Reason. And I should remind you that you have also promised to tell us more about the "things-in-themselves."

KANT: It just so happens that I can do both at once. The other functions of reason to which I referred are the *practical* functions.

BW: So now we are beginning to talk about the second *Critique,* the *Critique of Practical Reason?*

KANT: Yes. Let me answer your previous question by saying that our contact with the things-in-themselves is a matter of *practice,* not a matter of knowledge.

BW: I am afraid I don't understand.

KANT: Only part of our lives is spent *observing* the world, trying to organize our experience into knowledge. And it is only as observers that we raise the question, is the world as we know it the same as the world is "in itself"? In the realm of action, on the other hand, this question doesn't arise. As a scientist, I can ask myself whether I *really* understand the chemical structure and properties of this wine I am drinking; but as a nonscientist, I simply drink and enjoy it unquestioningly.

BW: "I drink, therefore I am"?

KANT: [*smiles appreciatively*] Or is it, "I think, therefore I drink"?

BW: [*laughs*] So knowledge of things-in-themselves comes through practical reason?

KANT: No, not *knowledge.*

BW: Oh. Well then, is that why you insist that we can't know the world "in itself," or know God, or know about the immortality of the soul?

KANT: That's right, but to say that we can't *know* about such things is not to say that there aren't right and wrong principles to be believed and avoided. It is not to say that belief isn't *rational.*

BW: So you would say that we can't know that God exists, but it is rational for us to believe in Him?

KANT: Precisely.

BW: But doesn't this mean that we live in two worlds at once—a world of nature and knowledge and a world of action and belief?

KANT: Yes, I call these the *"sensible"* world and the *"intelligible"* world, respectively. But it is important not to think that these are actually two *different* worlds; they are one and the same world, known on the one hand through experience, *acted in* on the other. Sometimes I refer to them as two different *"standpoints."* It is a question of the way in which we are conceiving of the world at any given time, that is, as something to be known, or as a stage on which something is to be performed. Most of the time, of course, we adopt both standpoints, more or less together.

BW: We have gained a pretty good idea about the first standpoint —the standpoint of knowledge; please tell us more about the second standpoint, the standpoint of practical reason.

KANT: I can summarize it in one word: *morality.* The key to practical reason is our concept of morals.

BW: What is morality? I know you mean by it such principles as "thou shalt not kill" and "don't cheat on your exams," but how do you define morality as such?

KANT: In a word, morality is *duty.* In a sentence, morality is a set of unconditional principles, valid for everyone everywhere, which tell us what we *ought* to do.

BW: Valid for everyone everywhere?

KANT: Yes, it is hardly a moral principle if it is simply a matter of custom in one society, such as a rule of etiquette or the rule that one should keep one's carriage to the right on the road. A German in 1790 can condemn an action of a Persian in the fourth century B.C., or an American in 1982, for that matter, and if it is a moral question, it is perfectly right that he should do so. I can, and indeed it is my duty to, condemn wanton cruelty, for example, as immoral, wherever and whenever and no matter what the circumstances.

BW: You said that morality is a set of *unconditional* principles. What does that mean?

KANT: It means that they have no "conditions," and that there is never any set of circumstances that will excuse a person from his or her duty. In the second *Critique,* I call these principles *"categorical imperatives."* An "imperative," of course, is just a command, an order. "Categorical" means the same as "unconditioned"; a categorical imperative orders us: *do this!* or *don't do this!* It doesn't say, "if you want to keep your friends, don't lie" or "if you want people to trust you, don't steal." I call those *"hypothetical* imperatives" or "conditional imperatives," because they apply only if you also accept the condition stated in the "if" clause.

BW: So, in your last example, if I don't care whether people trust me or not, the hypothetical imperative "if you want people to trust you, don't steal" doesn't apply to me.

KANT: Right. But of course the categorical imperative, "don't steal," applies to you all the time, no matter what you want.

BW: Therefore, a moral principle has to be categorical, unconditional, and apply to everyone, regardless of the circumstances, right?

KANT: Yes, except that the circumstances often have to be taken into account in the moral law itself. For example, whether or not taking something is an act of stealing depends on the circumstances —whether the thing is yours or not, whether it clearly belongs to someone else, whether it is or is not private property, and so on. Taking some pebbles from the beach is not stealing, but taking a handful of small stones from a jeweler will be—if they are not a gift, if you are not prepared to pay for them, and so on.

BW: Who decides what is or is not a categorical imperative? God? Society?

KANT: That is precisely the main point of my entire philosophy, of course; no one decides for anyone else, not even God. We all decide for ourselves, or rather, it is reason, practical reason, that decides. The main principle of morality is that we are all *autonomous:* the moral law is in each of us, and through reason we can find it for ourselves.

BW: Then that is why you are so confident that morality must be the same for everyone everywhere?

KANT: Yes, because reason is universal . . .

BW: Like the categories of the understanding.

KANT: Yes, and it is for this reason too that morality must consist of laws which are unconditional, categorical. If there were conditions, these might vary from society to society, from case to case, and there could be no moral law. But morality consists of the dictates of practical reason, and there can be no conditions.

BW: Hence you believe, as Jean–Jacques Rousseau believed—did he not? —that in every one of us there is a deep moral sensibility, a sense of compassion for other people, the desire to do what's right.

KANT: You are right that Rousseau is very much my ideal here, much as Newton was in the realm of scientific knowledge. But we disagree about one essential feature; I do not want to relegate morals to sensibility, or to feelings of any kind. David Hume, you know, also argued such a view, that morality is a matter of passion and sentiment, not reason. I think such views are dangerous, because feelings can change. Feelings are conditional. If a whole society comes to feel that it is right to murder old people, or to fornicate with anyone and everyone, that doesn't make it right. Morality is a matter of reason, and reason is not always well served by sentiments.

BW: But isn't *feeling* important for morality? I mean, isn't the good person one who *wants* to do his or her duty?

KANT: Ah, yes, but you have hit on a very touchy topic. You assume that only feeling, desires and the like—which I simply summarize as *personal inclinations*—can motivate us to act. But I believe that practical reason itself can also motivate us; we sometimes do our duty for duty's sake and not because we want anything further or because we feel any particular way. In fact, we often do our duty despite the fact that we don't want to do it, and we measure a person's moral worth by just such cases.

BW: But isn't it much better when our inclinations and our duty coincide?

KANT: Of course; ideally, in a "holy" person, for example, all of one's personal inclinations will coincide with duties dictated by impersonal practical reason. This is rarely the case for any of us, but I try, at least. Because we are so often torn between personal desires and duty, we have to distinguish between acts done for the sake of inclination—even when they are in accordance with duty—and acts done for the sake of duty alone, against our inclinations.

BW: Are you saying that I am more morally worthy when I visit my grandmother, which is my duty, if I despise her, than when I visit my grandmother because I enjoy spending time with her?

KANT: It is an unfair example, of course, but yes, in terms of moral worth, which is all that we are talking about, the first case is better than the second. But of course everyone would be much happier in the second case.

BW: But you do make it sound as if a person is morally better when he or she acts for duty and for duty's sake alone.

KANT: It is unfortunate, perhaps, but there is in us this perennial conflict between what we want to do and what we ought to do. Looking on the bright side, however, it is one of the wonders of rationality that we alone, among all creatures on earth, are capable of acting purely out of reason, even against our inclinations.

BW: But wouldn't you prefer that this conflict didn't exist, so that people always wanted to do what is right?

KANT: Of course.

BW: Let me ask you a different kind of question in which we accept the fact that a person doesn't always get the opportunity to do his or her duty; circumstances interfere. In your system, which insists that circumstances aren't to be taken into consideration, are people who try but fail to do their duty considered immoral?

KANT: Good question. No, in my second *Critique* I explicitly insist that the only thing that is good without qualification is a *good will*. In other words, it is the *intention* that counts; a person can't be responsible for all the things that can go wrong. A person can only be completely responsible for what he or she *tries* to do.

BW: And this goes back to your statement early in the interview that *freedom* has to be the presupposition of moral responsibility; a person can't be held responsible for circumstances beyond his or her control, but a person is *always* responsible for his or her own decisions or acts of will.

KANT: Yes. And that is true even though one can never know what ulterior inclinations lurk below the surface of any decision.

BW: That sounds much like the theory of "unconscious motives" which will be argued more than a century from now by Sigmund Freud.

KANT: Who? Oh well, I'm glad to have been the originator, if that will help your audience appreciate my ideas.

BW: Let me go back to an earlier question; if everyone has the ability to find out for himself or herself what is right and what is wrong, and if our feelings are not allowed to play any role in this, how then do we decide what to do, what our duties are?

KANT: I don't want to say feeling is "not allowed"; in a particular situation, often the best thing to do is to follow one's feelings, but whether those feelings are *right* or not depends on reason. As to your question, how do we know what our duties are, we have to go back and consider why it is important that the principles of morality be universal, unconditional, formal principles, so that, through reason alone, without appealing to particular customs, feelings or circumstances, we can figure out what can be a categorical imperative and what cannot be.

BW: How *do* we figure that out?

KANT: The basic answer is this: you take what I call the "maxim" of your action, that is, a brief description of your intention, and you generalize it. You ask yourself, "what would happen if I were to make the maxim of my action a universal principle, for everyone else as well?"

BW: It sounds like something my mother used to say—"what if everyone else were to do what you're planning to do?"

KANT: You too have a wise mother! Well, you generalize your maxim, and if it doesn't hold up, you have to reject it. If it holds up, on the other hand, you might well have found a categorical imperative. To test it further, take its opposite, generalize it, and see what you get.

BW: For example, I generalize my intention to lie, and ask, "what if everyone were to lie?" I see that if everyone were to lie, no one would know whether anyone were telling the truth and no one would believe anyone, so you couldn't lie any more, because no one would believe anything anyway.

KANT: Very good. And the opposite maxim, "tell the truth," can be generalized without any such contradictions. Therefore, "tell the truth" is a categorical imperative, but "tell lies" could not be.

BW: But I can think of some pretty awful consequences of everyone's telling the truth, too. What about all the people who would be hurt if we couldn't tell "white lies," if we felt it our duty to tell people who are ugly that they are ugly and people who tell bad jokes that their jokes are bad and hostesses who can't cook that their sauerbraten tastes like mud pies?

KANT: But bad consequences are not part of the test. I am perfectly willing to concede that any action, however good, will have bad consequences in some instances. But notice that what happens in your lying example is not just bad consequences; the very act itself is undermined and no longer makes any sense.

BW: So it is the *logical* consequences you are looking for?

KANT: Yes, the test of a categorical imperative is whether it can *logically* stand up to generalization, whether it can serve as a standard of duty for all mankind.

BW: But suppose for example all the soldiers in a war were to refuse to fight. Then there would be no war, so no one could refuse to fight. Does that mean that it would be immoral for a young man to refuse to fight in a war, but moral for him to do so?

KANT: A good question. What you have shown is that we have to be very careful about what will count as a logical contradiction and, also, about the circumstances of war.

BW: You said before that circumstances sometimes entered into the formulation of the moral law itself, as, for example, in deciding what would count as stealing, remember?

KANT: Yes.

BW: Well, suppose we agree that no one should ever steal. But let's imagine that I am walking along jeweler's row on Sixth Avenue in New York and I see a diamond brooch lying on the sidewalk, right in front of a shop door. I pick it up; no one sees me. Now I agree that I ought not to steal, but what I want to know is, would it be stealing to walk away with the brooch rather than take it into the shop from where it most likely was lost?

KANT: But why should the moral principle have to decide that for you?

BW: Because you said that morality was a matter of universal, unconditional formal principles. But what good are universal principles if you don't know how to apply them in particular cases? The whole idea behind morality as you conceive it is that I can *rationally* decide what to do, what my duty is. But now it begins to look as if I have to make all the decisions personally after all, according to my immediate feelings, or according to what most people around me think I ought to do. How can I use the general principle in a particular case?

KANT: Well, for one thing, you can render the principle more specific; instead of asking, "should I steal?" you can ask, "should I walk away with this brooch which has probably been dropped by someone in this shop?"

BW: Ah, yes, but then suppose I qualify my maxim even more and ask, "should a philosophy student named Barbara from Texas walk away with *this* precise piece of jewelry from *this* shop on Sixth Avenue?". This has no consequences at all when it is generalized because I am the only person who could ever be in that position.

KANT: But of course a generalization can't include specific items, personal names, particular shops, and so on.

BW: But I can delete all of those and still make the description, although general, so specific that it can apply only to me in this single case.

KANT: No doubt you can, but then you are no longer finding moral laws; you are simply making up excuses.

BW: But doesn't this place all the weight of your theory on the formulation of the maxims themselves, rather than on the generalization?

KANT: It is a good objection, but more clever than fatal for my theory. You see, the generalization argument isn't the only formulation of the categorical imperative. There are other formulations as well.

BW: For example?

KANT: A categorical imperative must always treat people as *ends* and take their interests into consideration; it must never treat them merely as means, as a way in which to gain what you want from them.

BW: Or what we call "using people."

KANT: Yes, and a categorical imperative has to take into account the system of ends that make up practical reason, the good of *humanity,* our ability to live together in peace and common understanding.

BW: So it is ultimately humanity in general, rather than just the circumstances of any particular moral incident, that is the basis of your moral philosophy?

KANT: Yes; humanity is everything. My second *Critique* places too much emphasis on the formal restraints of morality; some day I want to write another book which will say more about the *application* of moral principles and the ends of humanity, and this will take care of your counter-examples too.[7]

BW: If your morality is ultimately about humanity, then how do God and the immortality of the soul fit into your philosophy?

KANT: They are what I call "postulates of practical reason." Freedom is such a postulate too. My argument is that one cannot be rational, that is, cannot be moral, unless he or she accepts these postulates as well.

BW: We have talked about freedom already; but why can't a person be rational without believing in God and immortality?

KANT: Well, so far I have argued a rather pure version of practical reason, in which I submit that a person ought to do duty for duty's sake. But, of course, this is overidealized. Suppose, for example, a man who always does what he is supposed to do suffers repeated misfortune, while his neighbor, who is thoroughly immoral, continually prospers. Is it rational for the former man to continue to do his duty for duty's sake alone, when it is obviously getting him nowhere, and when vice is apparently so much more lucrative?

BW: I suppose not.

KANT: *Unless,* of course, he also believes that *in the long run* his virtue will be rewarded and his neighbor's vices punished.

BW: I see.

KANT: Thus, to be rational he must also believe that virtue will

7. The book is *The Metaphysics of Morals,* published in 1797.

be rewarded and vice punished, even though it is also obvious that, in this life, such an ideal correlation does not always work out.

BW: And therefore he must believe in God and the afterlife, in order to believe in eventual reward?

KANT: Right.

BW: Doesn't that conflict with your idea about duty for duty's sake? Isn't the man then actually doing his duty with his eye on the divine reward?

KANT: Yes, I admit that there is a tension there; I'm working on it.

BW: But you said earlier that you considered yourself a fairly orthodox Christian. Believing in God and an afterlife does sound like being a Christian, but what about all the other doctrines of Christianity: the Trinity, the divinity of Jesus, the Immaculate Conception, Original Sin, the role of the church?

KANT: As a matter of fact, I have begun a book on that now, which will be an extension of my views in the second *Critique*.[8] The basic idea, which is in the *Critique* too, is that religion must be *rational,* and rational here means necessarily believed in, in order to be moral.

BW: What about *faith?*

KANT: Oh, I believe in faith, but faith doesn't mean some ignorant feeling which insists on accepting what we otherwise know to be false. Faith is rational; it can be defended by good reasons, *moral* reasons.

BW: Namely, that you can't be moral if you don't also believe in God and immortality.

KANT: Right.

BW: But what about the other Christian doctrines?

KANT: They are rational insofar as they must be believed in order to be moral.

BW: Are they?

KANT: Some are, some are not. Belief in miracles is never rational. Miracles contradict the cause-and-effect laws of science. Belief in the existence of Jesus as a moral example is rational. He was indeed a holy person.

BW: It sounds as if you might be heading for trouble; that doesn't sound very orthodox to me.

8. *Religion within the Bounds of Reason Alone,* published in 1793.

KANT: So far, I haven't had any problems with my views.[9]

BW: Time is running short, so I think it is time to move to your third *Critique,* the *Critique of Judgment,* which has just been published. We certainly want to hear about that, but first, we have a word from our local stations.

*   *   *

BW: Professor Kant, tell us what your third *Critique* is about.

KANT: It is an attempt to systematize the first two *Critiques* and bring them into some larger, more unified vision of the universe. In terms of knowledge—let us say, a scientific investigation—the theory of the first *Critique* is perfectly adequate; in terms of the problems of morality and the rational defense of religion, the groundwork of the second *Critique* is, I think, the right starting point for the investigations I am now conducting into particular moral problems and religious doctrines. But what is still missing is a sense of how they fit together, of an overall sense of our place in the universe, of the role of knowledge and the purpose of virtue and religious belief.

BW: And that is what the third *Critique* tries to do?

KANT: I think it *does* do this, but I am afraid that many people who like my first two *Critiques* may not like the third.

BW: Why is that?

KANT: Because it is much more speculative, I would almost say more "romantic" or more "mystical," even if it is systematic. It doesn't have the hard and fast concepts and principles of the first two books; in fact, the whole thesis of the third *Critique* turns on a metaphor, a metaphor that we *rationally* have to accept, but a metaphor, nonetheless.

BW: And what is that?

KANT: It is the vision of a *living* universe, not the lifeless mechanism of Newtonian mechanics, but a purposeful, growing cosmos, a divine cosmos, one much like that many of the ancient philosophers suggested.

BW: But isn't this just the kind of metaphysics—a view of the way things *really* are "in themselves"—that you rejected in the first *Critique?*

KANT: No, what I rejected and still reject is the idea that we can *know* any of this; that is why I call it a metaphor. It is the idea

9. In 1793, in fact, he would be censored by the government.

that the universe is a divine unity, a living creation, in which all of our knowledge can be ultimately unified and we approach the absolute truth, in which all our actions add up to something significant under the auspices of a divine principle. I cannot imagine believing otherwise! Why seek knowledge if you don't also believe that it is ultimately on the way to truth, if you don't believe that the universe ultimately can be explained? Why seek virtue if you think that life is ultimately meaningless, that the universe is simply indifferent to our sense of justice and morality?

BW: You would be very unhappy with a great many twentieth-century physicists and philosophers, Professor.

KANT: Why, what do they . . . ? Never mind, I don't want to know. At least I won't be alive to listen to them. Besides, I have my own cynics and irrationalists right here in Königsberg to deal with. But, irregardless, that is the culminating vision of my philosophy.

BW: But it isn't knowledge?

KANT: No, it consists of what I call "regulative ideas," that is, ideas that we have to rationally accept, but which remain a matter of faith. They can't be proved; but they must be believed.

BW: Tell me what you mean by a living, purposeful universe.

KANT: The concept that concerns me in the third *Critique* is *teleology*. The word comes from the Greek: *telos* means purpose, teleology means purposiveness. A teleological explanation is an explanation in terms of purposes. For example, I can explain why a camel has a hump by saying, "in order to allow it to store water for long periods of drought." Notice that I explained the animal's structure by giving its purpose, not by explaining its causes. In fact, in biology in general, it is almost always easier and more informative to give a teleological explanation in terms of purposes rather than a causal explanation in terms of antecedent conditions. Perhaps some day scientists will be able to explain living things in terms of causes only, but I tend to be cautious about this. Anyway, today we cannot do so, and teleological explanations remain the explanatory principle of living things.

BW: You make it sound as if a causal explanation would be more desirable, but until we have one we will make do with teleology.

KANT: I do think we can only improve our knowledge of nature as we broaden the scope of our causal accounts, even to living things. But I do not think that teleological accounts are therefore inferior; in fact, the whole purpose of the third *Critique* is to defend the importance of teleology and to present a cosmological vision of the universe itself as a teleological system.

BW: ⁻ What is the purpose of the universe, Professor Kant?

KANT: A presumptuous question, I should say, and any answer would no doubt be even more presumptuous. [*smiles*] I don't know that you can really give a satisfactory answer to that question. Suppose I were to ask you to tell me the purpose of some animal's existence—a dog or a camel, let's say. How would you respond? You can explain various features of the animal by showing how they aid its survival, but what would you say if I asked you the purpose of its survival itself? Or the purpose of the species? Or of life itself?

BW: I'm not really sure what I could say.

KANT: And so it is with the universe. It is teleological, but it is purposiveness without a purpose. There is no goal, certainly no conscious goal. God, of course, knows all of this, but we do not, cannot. We can only believe—must believe—that the universe has its own intrinsic purposes, and these are better understood by the artists and poets than by the philosophers and scientists.

BW: You mentioned that the third *Critique* is also a theory of art; how does that fit into teleology?

KANT: Art, too, is a purposive activity which has no ultimate purpose. The artist works hard for his final creation, but it would be vulgar to ask, why do it? It is the creative act itself that counts, and I see God and the universe in that way too: an artist and his creation, divine purposiveness but without an ulterior purpose.

BW: You know, of course, that some of the great poets of Germany—Goethe in particular—have taken the vision of your third *Critique* very much to heart.

KANT: I am not at all surprised. As I said, it is primarily a poetic image, and I also say some flattering things about poetic geniuses, which I am sure Herr Goethe will appreciate. In fact, I have been corresponding with a young friend of Goethe's, Friedrich Schiller,[10] who has some rather interesting ideas about the education of mankind through art and poetry, and my philosophy.

BW: I must say, I am surprised. You are considered the greatest rationalist thinker in the modern world, and here you are talking about the genius of poets and the universe as a grand metaphor.

KANT: Yes, I know, but here among my colleagues, many of whom tend toward some sort of Gothic mysticism and irra-

10. Johann Christoph Friedrich Schiller (1759-1805), German poet and playwright and a devoted follower of Kant and friend of Goethe.

tionalism, I surely am a super-rationalist. We shall see what time will say of me and my faith in reason. Your viewers in the twentieth century will probably never hear of Hamann, or Herder, or the other enemies of the Enlightenment. My philosophy will last for centuries, you'll see.

BW: That is why we are here, Professor Kant. Let me ask you one last personal question: have you ever considered leaving Königsberg, traveling around Europe as something of an international hero?

KANT: No. Of course, I would love to see Paris, but change frightens me. I like it here, and I always have. Königsberg is a cosmopolitan seaport, and I can pretty much see all of the variety of humanity here, which only supports my view that everyone is ultimately the same—that is, human. Besides, I am already an old man, and I still have much work to do. So I will stay at home, keep on teaching at the University and write philosophy.

BW: Thank you, Professor Immanuel Kant.

KANT: Thank *you,* and I appreciate this opportunity to speak to you Americans of a future century.

BW: And now, this is Barbara Wahrheit, for DBS news, on special assignment in Königsberg, East Prussia, saying good night to the eighteenth century and to Professor Immanuel Kant. And happy birthday, Professor! Stay tuned to these same stations for an update on the latest developments in France, coming to you direct from the National Assembly in Paris.

Part II A Post-Kantian Symposium (13 February 1804)

Good evening. This is Barbara Wahrheit, speaking to you from the University at Jena, where we have just been attending a memorial service for the great philosopher Immanuel Kant, who died yesterday in Königsberg at the age of seventy-nine. Professor Kant leaves behind him what has to be the greatest philosophical legacy of modern times. There is not a poet nor an intellectual in Germany who has not been deeply affected by his work, and in his memory, we have hurriedly put together a symposium of some of the most influential thinkers in Germany, to tell us about their reactions to Kant and the new directions in which they are taking his critical philosophy. We hope that this will be a fitting tribute to the man who has made Germany the center of philosophical life in Europe, probably for the rest of the nineteenth century.

We are sorry to announce that two of our invited speakers regret that they are unable to join us in honoring Professor Kant tonight. Friedrich Schiller, the great playwright, tells us that he is very ill and desperately trying to finish his latest play, *Wilhelm Tell,* which he describes as a Kantian drama of freedom. We also regret that the great poet Johann Goethe will not be with us. He explained to me that despite his great admiration of Kant, he thinks himself too poor an abstract thinker to do justice to the great philosopher.

With us tonight are six of the leading intellectual lights of German letters. All of them have expressed an abiding debt of gratitude to Immanuel Kant and many of them are beginning to call themselves "German Idealists," to express their allegiance to the late Professor. They are:

> [*camera pans across the long table, then pans back and dollies in for tight close-up of each panelist as he is introduced*]

Johann Fichte from Berlin, the most controversial of the neo-Kantians, was fired from the University of Jena in 1799 on a charge of atheism. And yet he sees his entire philosophy as an extension and a systematization of Kant's *Critiques.* He became instantly popular throughout Germany, in fact, when his first published book, *Critique of All Revelation,* was mistaken for Kant's new book on religion, back in 1792. By the time the mistake was corrected, Fichte had become a celebrity. He summarized his own views in his *Science of Knowledge (Wissenschaftslehre),* which has gone through several editions and revisions since 1794 to become one of the most influential books of the decade.

43

On Professor Fichte's right is **Friedrich Schelling** from the University of Wurzburg, formerly professor at the University of Jena. Herr Schelling is the bright new star of German Idealism, who was offered a professorship at Jena at age twenty-three, when he had already published a half dozen books. He was once a close friend and disciple of Fichte, but he has now moved off in new directions, which I hope he will be willing to tell us about.

Next, we are pleased to introduce **Karl Leonard Reinhold,** professor of philosophy at Kiel University, who claims that his philosophy of "rational realism" is much more faithful to Kant than the new "idealism." We are told that an exciting battle is shaping up between the German Idealists and the more conservative Kantians such as Professor Reinhold. Professor Reinhold was once a student of Fichte himself, but he has recently attacked the younger idealists, particularly Schelling. And they have responded in kind. So this may turn out to be a lively evening as well as a fitting tribute to Kant.

Next, we meet **Friedrich Heinrich Jacobi,** who comes to us from the Academy of Sciences at Munich. He was a businessman for a while, but always considered himself first and foremost a philosopher. He has particularly upset many of the orthodox Kantians by taking Kant as a purely subjective idealist. Jacobi believes that Reality cannot be known or understood except through immediate feeling and belief, or *Glaube.* He has also upset the German Idealists by insisting that Kant's thought cannot be made into a coherent system, a goal busily being pursued by the Idealists.

Friedrich Schlegel is currently living in Paris as the editor of *Europa,* a literary magazine. He is the founder of *das Romantik* or *Romanticism,* which he bases on the philosophies of Fichte and Schelling. Herr Schlegel insisted that he is not a philosopher but a literary critic; it seemed to us appropriate, nonetheless, to include him here tonight. We have been warned, however, that there is some recent animosity between Schlegel and his one-time friend Schelling, who recently ran off with the wife of Schlegel's brother. Asked recently to define "Romanticism," Schlegel said, "Romantic poetry is progressive universal poetry. It shall not only unite all of poetry, but philosophy and rhetoric too. We will make poetry sociable and society poetic, and animate everything by the vibrations of humor."

Now we meet **G.W.F. Hegel,** currently a lecturer here at Jena. Herr Hegel is relatively unknown in the intellectual world but he has been highly recommended by Herr Schelling, and as the author of a harsh review of Reinhold (in the *Critical Journal of Philosophy,* which he edited with Schelling until last year) we thought it might be interesting to have him here tonight.

*   *   *

BW: Professor Fichte . . .

FICHTE: I'm not actually a professor at the moment.

BW: Herr Fichte, you probably knew Kant better than anyone else here tonight; tell us something about him.

FICHTE: Well, as you know, it was Kant who gave me my first big break and secured for me the chair at Jena. But as I became more popular, Professor Kant seemed to feel threatened by me and offended that I should suggest any changes in his supposedly eternal system. You may also know that in 1799 Kant published a rather unjust letter in which he declared that he was astounded that anyone—namely me—should think that his philosophy was not completely finished and perfect.[1] So you see, with regard to his own work, which is how I knew him, Kant was not exactly generous.

REINHOLD: [*interrupting*] Perhaps that is because you betrayed him.

BW: [*slightly flustered, but chooses to overlook the interruption*] And you do think, Herr Fichte, that the Kantian system was imperfect and incomplete?

FICHTE: Definitely. I think in spirit it is indeed the best philosophy ever produced, but I think Kant was led astray by his love of Newton and science, and I think his emphasis on knowledge in the first *Critique* leads to disastrous consequences for the rest of his philosophy.

BW: For instance?

1. *Open letter on Fichte's* Wissenschaftslehre,
     August 7, 1799

   Public Declarations, No. 6; VOL. XII, *pp. 370-71*

. . . I hereby declare that I regard Fichte's *Theory of Science* [*Wissenschaftslehre*] as a totally indefensible system.
   I am so opposed to metaphysics, as defined according to Fichtean principles, that I have advised him, in a letter, to turn his fine literary gifts to the problem of applying the *Critique of Pure Reason* rather than squander them in cultivating fruitless sophistries.
   I renounce any connection with that philosophy.
   I must remark here that the assumption that I have intended to publish only a *propaedeutic* to transcendental philosophy and not the actual system of this philosophy is incomprehensible to me. Such an intention could never have occurred to me, since

FICHTE: Well, most of all, there is an intolerable split between the world of knowledge and the world of free action; in the first world we see ourselves as simply knowers, and we see the world, including ourselves, as mere objects completely determined by the laws of cause and effect. In the second world, we see ourselves as free agents bound by the universal moral law. But Kant nowhere ties these together, and we are left with two completely different and contradictory views of ourselves and our place in the world.

BW: But didn't Kant bring these two together—or what you call "systematize" his philosophy—in the third *Critique,* the *Critique of Judgment?*

FICHTE: No. He may have claimed to do so, but the objectivity of knowledge and the primacy of Newtonian mechanics remains uncompromised.

BW: What do you believe must be done then to save the "spirit" of Kant's philosophy? What have you done with his system?

FICHTE: I believe that I have extracted its true kernel, which is *freedom.*

JACOBI: I agree!

SCHELLING: I too!

FICHTE: What links the first *Critique* with the second is the concept of free activity: in the first case, the activity of applying concepts and positing (constituting) the world; in the second, the activity of the will in deciding what is right and trying to do it. The key to the system is thus this notion of free activity of the transcendental self, or what I sometimes call simply "self-activity." Ultimately, everything is self–identical, or "$A = A$".[2]

I took the completeness of pure philosophy within the *Critique of Pure Reason* to be the best indication of the truth of my work.

There is an Italian proverb: May God protect us from our friends, and we shall watch out for our enemies ourselves. There are friends who mean well by us but who are doltish in choosing the means for promoting our ends. But there are also treacherous friends, deceitful, bent on our destruction while speaking the language of good will . . . and one cannot be too cautious about such men and the snares they have set. Nevertheless the critical philosophy must remain confident of its irresistible propensity to satisfy the theoretical as well as the moral, practical purposes of reason, confident that no change of opinions, no touching up or reconstruction into some other form, is in store for it; the system of the *Critique* rests on a fully secured foundation, established forever; it will be indispensable too for the noblest ends of mankind in all future ages.

IMMANUEL KANT

(from A. Zweig, ed., *Kant's Philosophical Correspondence*)

2. See footnote 3, p. 18.

Once you recognize this, then Kant's two worlds of knowledge and free action are not two *worlds* at all, but simply two different views of ourselves and the world.

BW: But Kant sometimes said they were two "standpoints."

FICHTE: Yes, but he thought you necessarily adopted both of them. I see them rather as a *choice;* one can either view the world as a Newtonian machine, with ourselves as mere objects and victims of the laws of nature, *or* one can see himself as a moral agent, defender of the moral law, for whom the world is nothing but a stage on which we can act out our ethical struggles.

BW: Which view is the correct one?

FICHTE: Correct? I said one must *choose,* and the sort of philosophy one chooses depends on the kind of person one is. A philosophical system is not just a piece of furniture that one buys or throws away at will; it is rather animated by the soul of the person who holds it.

BW: Do you have a preference yourself then, Herr Fichte?

FICHTE: Of course; I prefer the moral viewpoint. The objective view, which holds the world of knowledge and ourselves as mere objects, I consider dogmatic and dehumanizing. It is a view that assumes that the world is just *there* for us, and we are just "there" too, as observers, as peculiar objects, but no more. The other view, which I call "idealism," invites us to accept ourselves as moral agents and accept *responsibility* for the way the world is. There is no question in my mind which viewpoint is superior.

BW: And what about the world itself? Doesn't it exist for you?

FICHTE: Of course it exists! It is a question of *how* it exists, for what *purpose.* And I say that the world exists in order for us to exert our moral wills, to present obstacles to be overcome, to accept causes to be fought and fights to be won.

BW: But do we "constitute" the world, as in Kant's philosophy?

FICHTE: Yes, but not as objects for knowledge; we "posit" the world as an opposition to ourselves, as something to struggle in and against. We posit ourselves; we posit the not-Self; and we come to see that the not-Self is nothing but the self.

BW: So everything in your philosophy, and you think in Kant's philosophy also, comes down to the self, to the "I"?

FICHTE: Yes, not an individual "I," of course, but rather an absolute Self, which produces everything. And the purpose of philosophy, accordingly, is to recognize that the seeming opposition between ourselves and the world is our own doing, and that our task in life, or what I call the "vocation of man," is to fight the good fight—the *moral* fight.

BW: I am sure you have been following the recent developments in France; do you look forward to the international battles that seem to be brewing?

FICHTE: Yes, I do, and I am hoping that one of the products of Napoleon's manipulations in the German provinces will be the birth of a German state.

BW: I see. Let me ask you one more question about your relationship to Kant's philosophy before we move on to the other speakers. You have said that the "thing-in-itself" is a travesty for the critical philosophy. What have you done with the "thing-in-itself"?

FICHTE: What have I *done* with it? Nothing at all. There is no such thing, and there is nothing in Kant's philosophy that requires it.

BW: What about the world of freedom?

FICHTE: Once you agree that it is the active Self that is ultimately real, why do you need a world-in-itself over and above the world experienced by the self in action?

BW: What about the passivity of sensations? They have to be caused by something, don't they?

FICHTE: Why? Don't you see that according to Kant's own view, causality is a concept *within* the world of experience and therefore can't be used to explain the world of experience itself. No, sensations, too, are posited by us as hypothetical components of experience. Whatever is necessary in experience is necessary for freedom, and for no other reason.

BW: Thank you Professor—er, Herr Fichte.

FICHTE: I am surprised.

BW: Why is that, Herr Fichte?

FICHTE: You are the first reporter who hasn't asked me if I am an atheist.

BW: Oh, *are* you an atheist, Herr Fichte?

FICHTE: No.

BW: Thank you again. [*turns to next guest as camera pans and comes in for tight close-up*] Professor Schelling, you have recently become a rather harsh critic of Herr Fichte's philosophy, although you seem extremely close to it. What are the differences in the ways in which you have systematized Kant?

SCHELLING: Thank you. Yes, I began as an enthusiastic disciple of Fichte. In fact, my first major work, *The "I" as the Principle of Philosophy,* is a direct extension of Fichte's work, as the title will tell you. I too take self-activity as the ultimate truth, and consider freedom to be both the beginning and the end of philosophy. But there the resemblance ends, even if some currently respectable philosophers can't tell the difference. [*Throws a scowl toward Reinhold, who is sitting next to him. Reinhold makes a hostile gesture in return*] What is wrong with Fichte's philosophy [*Fichte frowns*] is that he does not give nature and knowledge their due. Mother nature is not simply a "posit" of our moral selves; she is an independent existence and a source of marvel to anyone who does not find knowledge a tedious task compared to the heroism of revolution.

FICHTE: I object to . . .

BW: Please, Herr Fichte.

SCHELLING: So what I have done with Fichte's philosophy is to return it to the true spirit of Kant, which includes the appreciation of knowledge and nature as well as the moral law. "The starry heavens above, the moral law within," Kant said. But Fichte has sacrificed the heavens to the moral law.

BW: So you want to return to Kant's celebration of knowledge and Newton?

SCHELLING: No, not at all. I agree with Fichte that Newton is offensive to our spiritual conception of ourselves, and I think mechanical explanations of the sort Kant talks about in the first *Critique* are the lowest level of understanding nature, hardly worth the name. It is Kant of the third *Critique* whom I find exhilarating. For there Kant, like Goethe, with whom I have had extensive discussions on the topic, and like Leibniz, our great German predecessor, takes a view of nature as a living force, as a purposeful "teleological system." I do insist on a return to Kant and his appreciation of nature; but it is living nature, not dead mechanism, to which I want to return.

BW: Professor Schelling, you have become famous for the lectures you have been giving on science, which I understand include everything from physics and astronomy to zoology and psychology.

SCHELLING: Yes, I call this "the philosophy of nature," but it is not so eclectic as you make it sound. Indeed, the core idea of my philosophy of nature is to comprehend the whole of science according to a single basic concept.

BW: What kind of concept?

SCHELLING: In a word, *force.*

BW: Force?

SCHELLING: Yes, although my concept is not to be equated with Newton's mechanical concept of force (as mass times acceleration of a moving body). My concept of force ultimately means what we have called self-activity, a tendency to manifest itself, and this is to be found in everything from electricity and magnetism to the solar system and living things.

BW: Do you view the solar system as a living thing?

SCHELLING: Yes, I do.

BW: And the whole of nature, in the same manner?

SCHELLING: Yes I do, just as Kant did.

BW: But doesn't that put you back in the same position for which Herr Fichte criticized Kant, namely, a two-worlds view of nature and free action which cannot be brought together? [*Fichte nods heartily*]

SCHELLING: Not at all. I too take the principle of Self and self-activity to be primary, but I see this Self, which I call the "world soul" (*Weltseel*) developing in two different aspects—one as self-conscious Self, as "spirit," through philosophy, religion and art; the other as nature, which is also the self-development of the world-soul, but through matter, and not self-conscious.

BW: But these are ultimately the same?

SCHELLING: Yes, they are ultimately two aspects of one and the same Absolute self-activity.

FICHTE: An empty identity! It is a mere bandage over the problem of opposition! An excuse to avoid one's responsibilities and moral struggles and retreat to the transcendental luxuries of the university!

SCHELLING: Herr Fichte, just because I don't share your enthusiasm for clinking beer glasses and patriotic swords doesn't mean that I have left the world behind me.

BW: Professor Schelling, let me ask you what this "world-soul" is; is it God?

SCHELLING: Yes, you can certainly say that. But it is a God who is at one with his creation, and at one with all of us.

FICHTE: I was fired for saying that!

SCHELLING: Ah, yes, but that was because you were unfortunately less than sunclear[3] about the fact that it was not the individual

---

3. Fichte had recently published a book called "A Sunclear Report on the Latest Philosophy," an attempt to defend his *Wissenschaftslehre.*

ego that created the world, and you must admit that your God looks suspiciously like nothing more than the sum of human moral activity.

FICHTE: My God is the same as your God, the Absolute Self!

SCHELLING: Yes, but my God is also our creator, even if he is at one with his creation. God is the great artist who is creating himself, with nature as his material, infusing us all with his spirit. [*Schlegel is heard to shout something unintelligible*]

FICHTE: How can you get away with that!

SCHELLING: Because my piety has never been questioned.

BW: So, Professor Schelling, you see the universe as God creating Himself?

SCHELLING: Yes, I see art, not knowledge or moral action, as the highest form of human—and divine—activity; and I think this is what professor Kant intended in his third *Critique* as well.

BW: Well it certainly helps explain why you have become the patron philosopher of the romantic poets.

SCHELLING: Yes, I think poetic genius is the most divine human attribute. [*Schlegel gives a cheer*]

BW: Thank you, Professor Schelling. Professor Reinhold, I know you have some considerable disagreements with what has been said here so far.

REINHOLD: Yes, indeed I do. I see this squabbling between Herren Fichte and Schelling as a mere comedy of errors; their views are ultimately the same, and they are based on the same mistake—their very starting point, about which they are so cocksure. They assume that because philosophy begins with consciousness, there can be nothing other than consciousness. I say that they utterly confuse form and content. I agree that we supply *the form* to our experience through our own activities, but *the content* is given. There can be no content to our experience without empirical, sensory material, and their idea that somehow we supply this too is incomprehensible nonsense.

BW: But you do not deny the possibility that the "things-in-themselves" cause us to have sensations, which are the content of experience?

REINHOLD: No, I do not deny this, but I do not assert it either. What Kant has taught us are the limits as well as the possibilities for knowledge. He taught us how to practice "phenomenology," to describe the world of our experience and its necessary structures. The thing-in-itself, and the knowing subject too, are ultimately unknowable and inconceivable. The thing-in-itself is a pure abstraction, a "residue" of knowledge but itself not knowable.

BW: Would you say that you are doing psychology then?

REINHOLD: Emphatically not, nor ontology either. I am doing what Kant tried to do, to demonstrate the necessary features of experience. I should add that I am sorry that you have not thought it fitting to invite our Kantian colleague Jakob Fries, who is now in Heidelberg.[4] He has indeed turned Kant's program into a psychology, or perhaps what he calls an "anthropology," in which he rejects the idea that we can deduce the necessary structures of experience. I very much disagree with him, but he would be another welcome antidote to these egomaniacs who think the Self makes *everything* necessary.

BW: So you do not believe that the Self is absolute?

REINHOLD: That is utter nonsense too. There is nothing like that in Kant, and our dear departed Professor must be fuming in his coffin to know that these two charlatans have been broadcasting their travesties into the twentieth century.

SCHELLING: Travesties! You pedantic fraud, you know your only relationship to Kant is the fact that you licked his philosophical boots long enough to secure a professorship![5]

REINHOLD: You should talk!

SCHELLING: Goethe got me my chair; but I have proven myself worthy of it.

REINHOLD: You have proven yourself an able showman, you mean. You've published almost a dozen books in fewer years, all of them slapdash, all of them different; when are you going to decide that you really believe, if indeed you believe anything?

SCHELLING: You have your nerve—you are the monkish fox who started this whole business of "systematizing" Kant, and you are criticizing those of us who have actually done so. I agree with Herr Hegel's review of you: you are wholly unappreciative of the nature of philosophy and just want to make yourself famous with a system you can publish in Kant's shadows.

4. Jakob Friedrich Fries (1773–1843). Fries had recently published a polemical critique of Reinhold, Fichte and Schelling and had just completed his own revision of Kant's philosophy. He rejected the strong sense of "necessity" of Kant's first *Critique* and turned the critical philosophy away from its transcendental aspirations. Soon after this he accepted a professorship at Heidelberg.

5. The reader may be somewhat dismayed by the unprofessional and sometimes harsh language of the symposiasts in addressing one another. Please be assured that nothing is included here which they did not in fact say. The insults included here are their own; they are not fabricated. Much of their commentary can be better understood in light of their sometimes bitter competition.

REINHOLD: My system *is* a system, at least; it makes sense out of Kant, instead of that mystical mumbo-jumbo about nature as a "posit" of the Self or nature as God's creating Himself which you two are promulgating.

SCHELLING: You are just another dogmatist, as Fichte used that term; you are not a philosopher. You just assume the world exists, so why pretend to be a philosopher? Enough of your stupidities!

REINHOLD: I don't *assume* anything! I just insist . . .

BW: Gentlemen, gentlemen. Please!

REINHOLD: I just insist on mutual tolerance and freedom of inquiry; that's why I hate your idealism. It is only a matter of time until someone more powerful than you declares himself the sole spokesman for the Absolute.

BW: Professor Reinhold, you are well-known for your political liberalism; do you see a connection between Kant's philosophy and his abiding enthusiasm for the French Revolution?

REINHOLD: Indeed I do, and I myself was a continuing supporter of the revolution. It is the critical spirit that makes possible both Kant's great advance in philosophy and the enlightened atmosphere promised by the Revolution. My deepest regret is that that atmosphere has been poisoned by the kind of self-righteous tripe you have been listening to here. I agree that the philosophical problem of our time is the systematization of Kant, but that does not mean re-establishing the old philosophical dogmatism that Kant himself turned against and refuted.

SCHELLING: Are you calling us dogmatists?

REINHOLD: "If the shoe fits . . ."

FICHTE: Criticism presupposes authority; freedom presupposes limits.

JACOBI: I agree with Reinhold; your so-called "systems" smack of *pantheism*,[6] the denial of freedom, the denial of God, and a too-strong suggestion of authoritarianism.

BW: Herr Jacobi, you have been on record as opposing the whole attempt to "systematize" Kant; why is that?

JACOBI: Well, first, let's be clear what "systematize" means. We

---

6. Pantheism is the view that God is identical to the universe as a whole, but Jacobi was one of the philosophers in Germany to bring back the Dutch philosopher Spinoza (1632-1677), who was a determinist as well as a pantheist, and so the word took on harshly materialistic and atheistic connotations in German philosophy. Jacobi's preference for Kant, whom he opposed to Spinoza, was precisely because of Kant's emphasis on freedom and creativity, in the second and third *Critiques*.

have been throwing that term around as if it were something obvious to every schoolboy. But it is not; in fact, it is an arrogant and pretentious conception that finds no justification in Kant's own thinking. A system is a rational articulation of the whole of creation; an all-encompassing demonstration of the unity and purpose of the cosmos. Herren Fichte and Schelling, and Reinhold too, complain that Kant did not succeed in presenting us with such a "system" because he did not prove that our ultimate ideas about the universe are matters of knowledge. God, too, is not an object of knowledge, according to Kant. Well, I agree that Kant did not provide us with such a system, and for good reason: Kant showed once and for all that such a system is impossible. Herr Schelling, in particular, has argued as if Reason encompasses everything, but what Kant showed—and the very title *"Critique of Pure Reason"* proves this—is that reason has its limits, and the world as a whole cannot be rationally known. Thus a system is impossible, and there is no point in fighting about whose system is the "correct" one.

FICHTE: I agree that there are limits to knowledge, but are you saying too that we can have no moral contact with the world? That action alone determines our worth.

JACOBI: No, of course not. I agree with you that the first principle of philosophy is *freedom,* but I also think the world is *given* to us.

SCHELLING: But how then can we make sense of the idea that we do know the world as a unity, and as divine, as you yourself have often argued?

JACOBI: Through intuition, feeling, faith (*Glaube*). Kant showed us the limitations of reason; he didn't show us the limits of experience.

REINHOLD: You're wrong! Kant *did* argue the limitations of experience to the understanding and its application to sensibility.

JACOBI: Ah, that's playing with words. What would you call Kant's own vision of the universe as a living system, not mechanical but divine? He too believed in the experience of the Absolute, but he would not call it "knowledge." I would say that Kant, despite himself, emerges as a subjective idealist who denies that we can know anything, but at the same time tells us that we must believe. We enter the first *Critique* assuming the existence of the thing-in-itself as a cause of knowledge, but we leave the *Critique* having it taken away from us. What Kant simply left out was the most important ingredient in knowledge, not particular sensations or the "manifold of intuition" but the immediate intuition of the Absolute. He accused my friend Hamann—his friend, too—of "irrationalism," but it was Kant, ultimately, who ended up with irrationality—the idea that we could not know the world-in-itself, the Absolute, the universe as itself a divine, living system.

SCHELLING: I, too, would call this ultimate knowledge "intuition," but where intuition (*Anschauung*) or "*Glaube*" marks the end of philosophy to you it marks the beginning to me, for once one has this initial intuition of the Absolute, *then* one can begin to articulate it and demonstrate its various forms.

JACOBI: There is nothing to demonstrate. One intuits the divine unity, and that's it. All the rest is poetry.

SCHLEGEL: Hear, hear!

BW: Herr Schlegel, you obviously have some stake in this dispute.

SCHLEGEL: Yes I do, even though I do not pretend to be a philosopher. I have always admired old Kant, but I also regret that he wasted his genius by trying to be rational about everything. Indeed, I agree with Goethe that the only part of Kant's philosophy that is genuinely brilliant is the third *Critique,* where he not only proclaims quite rightly that the poetic genius is free from all rules, inspired by his sense of unity with the universe, but he himself manifests some of that same genius in his descriptions of the universe as a *Bildung,*[7] a development of infinity from finite matter. But it is not only that final vision, but rather the whole of the Kantian philosophy that should be seen as a metaphor, as an allegory of experience, a representation of the infinite in everything finite.

REINHOLD: What unintelligible garbage!

JACOBI: Let him finish; I agree with him.

FICHTE: *I* am *my* greatest creation.

SCHELLING: [*softly*] No, *I* am your greatest creation.

SCHLEGEL: I am an unabashed subjective idealist; I believe that everything is a creation of the self, and we poets are therefore the more highly developed specimens of consciousness. I think rationality is mere inhibition, a lack of imagination, servile obedience to the rules.

SCHELLING: Even Goethe insists that genius is "freedom within limitations."

SCHLEGEL: Yes, but Goethe has become an old fuddy-duddy and considers our romantic movement "sickly." Can you imagine? He was one of the poets who inspired our movement!

---

7. Literally, an education, self-cultivation.

FICHTE: Freedom doesn't mean anything unless it is bound by the moral law.

SCHELLING: You believe that because you have no appreciation for art, Herr Fichte.

SCHLEGEL: And because you have no appreciation for the infinite, Herr Fichte, no imagination, and no sense of humor.

FICHTE: I didn't come here to have my ideas insulted, or my person.

REINHOLD: I agree. Surely these young idealists should learn some manners.

SCHELLING: You two will never understand the nature of . . .

SCHLEGEL: Genius! The genius of modern poetry. The recognition of infinity within oneself!

BW: Herr Hegel, you have not said a word so far. Do you have anything to contribute to this somewhat rowdy discussion?

HEGEL: I am afraid I am not much of a public speaker, and I am not sure that I could say anything that my good friend Schelling has not already said much better. But I think the one dimension that has been left out of the discussion so far, an essential dimension for everything we have been talking about, is *history.* I have criticized Professor Reinhold for what I call his "historicism," his treatment of the history of philosophy as if it were nothing but an exhibit of mummies in a museum. He thinks he can begin philosophy from scratch and create a "system" all by himself, perhaps with some help from Kant. But I would make a similar comment about everyone here. I agree with Schelling that Fichte does not give due credit to nature, but I would argue too that he does not give enough attention to history, that freedom is not simply a given to be intuited, but has to be *developed,* fought for, and this has taken time, indeed, the whole of human history from the ancient tyrants of the Orient until the French Revolution and the modern constitutional state. Schelling, I know, has made a study of history as he has studied everything else, but I would argue that his philosophy does not take adequate account of development or what Schlegel called *Bildung,* however much he may say that his system is based on the notion of "self-activity."

SCHELLING: But surely you do not want to give so much emphasis to the random contingencies of history!

HEGEL: Even random contingencies may yet have some sort of logic. I agree that the business of philosophy is to demonstrate the absolute unity of the human experience, including knowledge of nature and free moral action. What I am saying is that it must also take account of historical development.

REINHOLD: I think Immanuel Kant would be sympathetic with that suggestion.

HEGEL: Yes. As you know, one of his last works was a small book on history and the development of freedom and morality. I would want to see Kant himself as part of that historical development now, and Herren Fichte and Schelling too.

SCHLEGEL: And *das Romantik* too.

HEGEL: No, I see romantic philosophy as self-indulgent digression from history, a distraction from the hard work of philosophy . . .

JACOBI: Now you are being too hard! Perhaps the "hard work of philosophy," as you put it, is not ponderous thinking but opening oneself up to the universe.

HEGEL: I do not believe that philosophy can make any claim to knowledge except through "the concept," that is, through articulate description of the various steps that have already been made in philosophy, by the Greeks as well as modern thinkers, on the road to absolute knowledge, that is, the single unified system of experience for which we have all been searching.

JACOBI: But I do not believe that there can be such a system.

HEGEL: That is why you will be seen as a digression in the progress of philosophy, whatever posterity might think of romantic poetry.

JACOBI: You have your nerve, for someone whose entire career in philosophy consists of serving as Schelling's apprentice.

HEGEL: I resent that!

SCHELLING: Perhaps I can defend you here, my friend, for we both know . . .

HEGEL: I can handle myself, thank you.

BW: Herr Hegel, can you give us a specific instance in which your view that history is important can illuminate our discussion.

HEGEL: Yes, there has been quite a controversy over who can quite properly call himself a Christian and who cannot, and as you know, Kant himself devoted his last, and in my opinion, perhaps his best book to this topic, his *Religion within the Bounds of Reason Alone.* But what Kant discusses very little, and what we have said nothing whatsoever about this evening, is the actual history of Christianity, the personality of Jesus and the fate of his religion. How can we decide what it is to be a Christian or to believe in God without any reference to the historical nature of the religion and the history of God Himself? This isn't just a question of pure or practical reason; it is also a question of *origins,* and what is living, what is dead, in Christ and Christianity.

SCHLEGEL: That I can accept. Jesus was a genius, too.

REINHOLD: That's blasphemous, but I agree that the history of religion is important. I also think that we must not forget that the whole purpose of the Reformation was to separate ourselves from the history of the Church, however, and to re-establish religion in ourselves, as a matter of personal faith.[8]

JACOBI: One of my colleagues has done some interesting work on this topic. Friedrich Schleiermacher, who is Professor of Religion at the University of Halle, has argued that Christian faith has nothing to do with reason or with history but is rather a separate faculty of feeling, an intuition that embraces "the All."

SCHLEGEL: I know him—he used to write for our journal.

SCHELLING: It sounds like your own philosophy, Jacobi.

JACOBI: Of course. But I think his research of the life of Jesus and the history of religion might interest you.

REINHOLD: Really?

HEGEL: Hrumph.[9]

BW: It seems that we've covered a great deal of territory, but we have strayed almost entirely from the subject of the evening, the philosophy of the late Immanuel Kant. So let me ask all of you, and please keep your answers brief, for your estimation of Kant's greatest contribution to Western thought. Herr Fichte?

FICHTE: The discovery of transcendental idealism, the absolute freedom of the ego in positing its own world.

SCHELLING: I agree, but I would add the discovery of the teleology of nature and the concept of purposiveness without purpose.

REINHOLD: The discovery of transcendental arguments and the overcoming of scepticism.

JACOBI: His "critique" of Reason.

SCHLEGEL: His suggestion that we can know the absolute through poetry.

REINHOLD: He didn't say that!

HEGEL: His discovery of "dialectic."

8. Reinhold's first major works were defenses of the Reformation and the secularization of religion.

9. Years later, Hegel would remark that Schleiermacher's view of religion as feelings of dependency made a dog a better Christian than any of us.

BW: What do you mean?

HEGEL: It's a long story. We probably shouldn't go into it here.

BW: Then let me ask you this, too: do you think Kant did or did not succeed in presenting us with a complete "system" of philosophy?

FICHTE: No, he did not. He ignored the absolute primacy of freedom.

SCHELLING: That's not true; he recognized as you never have the importance of nature, but he never figured out how to combine it with freedom.

FICHTE: But your empty identity won't do it either: you can't just *say* that nature is the same thing as consciousness.

BW: Please, gentlemen. Professor Reinhold, may we hear your views?

REINHOLD: I think that Professor Kant did have the correct idea for a system, but it needed to be worked out.

SCHELLING: [*sneering*] By you, presumably . . .

BW: [*quickly*] Herr Jacobi?

JACOBI: I do not think Kant tried to have a complete system, and that is his greatest virtue.

REINHOLD: But he himself tells us in his third *Critique* that philosophy is a system of theoretical and practical reason.

JACOBI: He was carried away by his rationalist enthusiasm, that's all.

BW: Herr Schlegel?

SCHLEGEL: Kant was a genius. He didn't need a system.

BW: Thank you. Herr Hegel?

HEGEL: I think Kant had the right idea but he still needs to be put into a complete system.

FICHTE: *I* did that!

SCHELLING: No, *I* did!

REINHOLD: *I* did!

HEGEL: [*softly*] You'll see, I *will*.[10]

BW: And because it seems to be one of the main themes of Kant's philosophy, let me ask what you think of the Self as the absolute point of departure for philosophy.

FICHTE: Of course; absolutely correct!

10. Hegel had just begun work on *The Phenomenology of Spirit,* perhaps his greatest book.

SCHELLING: Of course.

REINHOLD: Consciousness and reality as a polarity, yes, but Self alone, no.

SCHELLING: But that's what I mean, too!

REINHOLD: That's not what you *say!*

FICHTE: There is nothing in the ego that the ego doesn't put there itself.

JACOBI: I agree that the Self is everything, but philosophy doesn't much matter.

SCHLEGEL: Hear, hear!

HEGEL: Ah, but you make it sound as if the Self is just *there*. I say that Self—or "spirit"—has to evolve; it has to learn to recognize itself over a long, hard journey.

BW: And where do you think the Kantian philosophy will go from here, now that Kant is no longer with us to develop it himself?

FICHTE: It will become more political.

SCHELLING: It will become more creative.

REINHOLD: It will become more precise, if these clowns will leave it alone.

SCHELLING: If you weren't so much older than I am, I'd take you outside.

FICHTE: Now *that's* idealism in action.

REINHOLD: Idealist ruffians!

BW: Herr Jacobi, your prognosis?

JACOBI: Kant and Kantianism are about to become history.

BW: Herr Schlegel?

SCHLEGEL: Who cares?

HEGEL: I think that Kant is the basis and point of departure for the whole of modern philosophy. Nothing will proceed without him, but it will proceed, *to the Absolute!*

SCHLEGEL: I like your enthusiasm, if only you were a more interesting fellow.

HEGEL: Enthusiasm alone isn't worth much.

FICHTE: It's better than the academic tedium that most of you seem to think of as "philosophy."

REINHOLD: Am I the only rational philosopher left?

JACOBI, SCHLEGEL and SCHELLING [*together*]:   Let's hope so!

HEGEL: But we haven't yet decided what the purpose of the world is.

SCHLEGEL: Trust me, Herr Hegel, trust me.

REINHOLD: God help us.

FICHTE: Only those who help themselves.

SCHELLING: On with philosophy!

JACOBI: A silly game.

HEGEL: But it's the only game in town, Jacobi.

FICHTE: You haven't heard about Napoleon?

SCHLEGEL: What does the coarse Corsican have to do with poetry?

FICHTE: You'll see.

HEGEL: [*under his breath*] I suspect that we shall.

BW: Thank you, gentlemen. It is not often that a television interviewer gets a chance to meet not only one but a half-dozen spokesmen for the Absolute in a single meeting. For those of you who may be confused, "the Absolute" seems to mean just about "everything," and anything you want it to mean. But however much Professor Kant would have disagreed with much of what has been said tonight, it is his ideas and his defense of intellectual autonomy that made this gathering possible. In memory of the late Professor Immanuel Kant, this is Barbara Wahrheit, DBS news, signing off from Jena, February 13, 1804. And for those of you who missed the news earlier this evening, let me repeat that there are reports from Paris of still another plot to assassinate Napoleon Bonaparte; complete details on the eleven o'clock news later this evening. Stay tuned next for the first television performance of a new symphony by the young Viennese composer, Ludwig van Beethoven.

The sole thought which philosophy brings to history is the simple concept of Reason; *that Reason is the law of the world and that, therefore, in world history, things have come about rationally. . . . To him who looks at the world rationally the world looks rationally back.*

Hegel (Lectures on the Philosophy of History)

Part III G.W.F. Hegel (27 August 1770–14 November 1831)

An in-depth interview with veteran reporter Barbara Wahrheit in Berlin, 17 January 1820.

BW: Professor Hegel, the last time we met was in 1804, wasn't it? You certainly have accomplished a great deal since then.

HEGEL: Thank you. Yes, I remember that evening. Very interesting.

BW: Have you kept in touch with any of the other members on that distinguished panel?

HEGEL: Not really. Schelling and I fell out years ago. He's now teaching at Munich, but we don't correspond any more. Fichte is dead, so is Jacobi. Reinhold never was much of a colleague. Let's see, who else was there?

BW: Friedrich Schlegel.

HEGEL: Oh yes, he and his whole romantic crew have indulged themselves into a state of degeneracy, and without producing anything of great value, as we all suspected. Friedrich Scheirmacher is now my colleague in Berlin, as you probably know, but we don't talk much.

BW: Who are your friends here, Professor?

HEGEL: Oh, people from the government, lots of people from the university. I have some wonderful students; my wife and I give wonderful dinner parties. I am quite content with Berlin and my position here.

BW: I gather times have not always been so good for you in philosophy.

HEGEL: No, soon after that tribute to Kant I was promoted to assistant professor at Jena, but before I had a chance to establish myself Napoleon invaded us and the University was closed down.

BW: But you did publish one spectacular book that year, didn't you—*The Phenomenology of Spirit*?

HEGEL: Yes, in fact, I was putting the finishing touches on that work just as Napoleon came marching in.

BW: Did you see Napoleon?

HEGEL: Yes, I did. I think I wrote to a friend, "I have seen the world spirit on horseback," or something like that.

BW: Do you think the same of Napoleon now that he is in exile at St. Helena, his career finished and the empire dissolved?[1]

HEGEL: One doesn't talk very much about the old Emperor these days, you understand. To mention his name is to be suspected of "liberal tendencies." But to your audience in America I would say, times have changed, as they do. In 1806, with Napoleon on the march and everything uncertain, I wrote my *Phenomenology,* full of hope and enthusiasm. Now, in this period of peace, I feel as if everything's over, as if all that is left is for philosophy to paint its grey on grey and sift through the husks of an exciting history that is now over.

BW: You say "history is over"? Nothing will ever happen again?

HEGEL: Oh, of course history is not over, in that sense. But the great movements I foresaw in my *Phenomenology,* the unification of Europe and the resurrection of the ancient spirit of human harmony, those have been thwarted, at least for the moment. [*pause*] Of course, there will be other times; for example, I expect great things to happen in America, and soon too.

BW: I have heard that same expectation expressed by several of your colleagues; why is there such a great sense of future for America?

HEGEL: Well, our world is the old one; we have exhausted ourselves in wars and encrusted ourselves in seemingly indestructible fossils which we call our "culture." You and your world, the new one, you have another chance.

BW: After the University of Jena closed down and you published your *Phenomenology,* what did you do?

HEGEL: Oh God, then came the worst years of my life. I taught in a German high school, the Gymnasium at Nuremburg, for eight long years, and I mean l-o-n-g years. During that time, Napoleon conquered the world and lost it. I taught grammar and mathematics, as well as some philosophy and history, and I was bored, bored, bored.

BW: But didn't you also write a book on logic, which I have heard some people claim is the greatest innovation in the subject since Aristotle?

HEGEL: Yes, I wrote my *Science of Logic* during those years. It came out in 1812, or at least the first part did. I also put together the lecture outlines from my courses at Jena and published them just a few years ago as the *Encyclopedia of the Philosophical Sciences.*[2]

---

1. Napoleon died in exile the following year.

2. First edition, 1817.

BW: Then things started going well for you?

HEGEL: Very well, indeed. I received an offer from Heidelberg in 1816 which I accepted almost immediately. Then an offer came through from Berlin, where I really wanted to be, but it came too late. They made me another offer in 1818 which I couldn't refuse, and so I came here. I expect to stay here too; it's been a long road to success.

BW: Did you always want to be a philosopher, Professor Hegel? When you were a little boy could you imagine yourself becoming the most celebrated intellectual in Europe, along with such geniuses as Goethe and Kant?

HEGEL: Goodness, no! I never was a brilliant student. Interested and hard-working, yes, but hardly a genius. I just didn't have any ideas, or so it seemed to me then. You see, my two best friends in school . . .

BW: Where was that, Professor?

HEGEL: Tübingen, the theological seminary there.

BW: Were you studying to be a priest?

HEGEL: No, I went there because the state paid for my education. Besides, it's a Lutheran seminary . . . At any rate, my two best friends in school were Friedrich Schelling, whom you have met, and Friedrich Hölderlin, whom you have not. Schelling, as you probably remember, was a flamboyant genius who published entire books in the time it took me to do a single research paper. For years I was in his shadow; in fact, I didn't emerge until I published the *Phenomenology* in 1807. That was my declaration of independence. But I was already thirty-seven. Hölderlin was a genius too, but a poetic genius, from whom, I confess, most of my ideas came. He inspired us all. What an exciting fellow, a fantastic imagination . . .

BW: What has happened to Hölderlin?

HEGEL: I'm sad to say that he went completely mad—in 1804, I think—and he has been virtually a vegetable ever since. What a waste!

BW: I'm sorry to hear that.

HEGEL: Well, anyway, next to the two of them I always felt like an intellectual oaf. I fooled around with some ideas about the history of Christianity and its justifiability as a "rational" religion, but I didn't really sit down to write anything serious until 1799, when my father died. I received a small inheritance and decided that I'd try a university career.

BW: Did Schelling and Hölderlin help you?

HEGEL: Immensely. Hölderlin secured a tutoring job for me in Frankfort, and then Schelling recommended me for a job at the University of Jena, where he was teaching. You know the rest.

BW: Not exactly. Was the *Phenomenology* your first published work?

HEGEL: In a sense. I published some essays in a journal I edited with Schelling for a few years,[3] a piece on the difference between Fichte's and Schelling's philosophies, as a reply to their common enemy Reinhold.

BW: I recall reading about that lively conflict.

HEGEL: And then I wrote a critical piece on "faith and knowledge," mainly a discussion of Kant and a criticism of Jacobi. And then a short piece on scepticism; an essay on "natural law," but nothing memorable . . . For all intensive purposes, the *Phenomenology* was my first real work.

BW: What is the *Phenomenology* about?

HEGEL: Well, it's almost about everything! I began to write it as a book on logic and metaphysics, based on my lectures at Jena. I wanted to work out a "system," as I no doubt timidly announced at our last meeting, which would tie the whole of human knowledge together. It had three parts: logic and metaphysics; a philosophy of nature, or what you would call "science"; and a philosophy of spirit, or what you would call, "the humanities and social sciences."

BW: You finally did publish that in your *Encyclopedia,* right?

HEGEL: Right. But as I wrote the introduction to what was supposed to be the first volume—you know how these things happen—I let myself become somewhat carried away. The purpose of the introduction was to review the various moves that have been made in philosophy, trying to provide accounts of how it is that we know reality, culminating in my own view, which I more or less shared with Schelling, that no such account can be adequate unless it takes in the whole of reality and all of its inner connections. This is what we called "the Absolute".

BW: But you evidently didn't think Schelling had already done this, whereas he apparently thought that he had.

HEGEL: I know he thought that he had. But he was mistaken. Oh, he asserted the correct conclusion, "All is One," but that's hardly enough. My mystical students from southern Germany are uttering slogans like that all the time; that isn't philosophy.

BW: What did you accomplish that Schelling failed to do?

3. *Critical Journal of Philosophy,* 1801-03.

HEGEL: I actually demonstrated how we reach "the Absolute," namely, by showing how all of the moves made in the history of philosophy ultimately lead to this one conclusion.

BW: So the *Phenomenology* is actually a book about the history of philosophy?

HEGEL: Well, no. But also, yes. You see, philosophy and the history of philosophy are pretty much the same enterprise; the ideas that emerge through history in the great philosophers have similar relationships with one another when we take them out of historical context.

BW: I'm not sure I understand.

HEGEL: Consider, for example, the sequence of arguments in British empiricism: Locke insisted that all knowledge comes from experience; forty years later David Hume argued that because all knowledge comes from experience, we can never really know anything. But if we look at this historical progression, we can see that it also follows a kind of logic. The one set of ideas can be argued from the other, independently of the fact that a particular philosopher named Locke argued one and was followed in a few years by another particular philosopher named Hume.

BW: Thus you can talk about the logic of the ideas without naming any particular philosophers, and come out with the same order that one would find in history.

HEGEL: More or less.

BW: More or less?

HEGEL: It doesn't matter. If you were teaching a philosophy course, it might be very fruitful to compare an idea of, let's say, Plato, with a suggestion of Spinoza. It doesn't matter that they don't appear together in history or whether Spinoza ever worried about Plato.

BW: Are you saying, therefore, that the *Phenomenology* is a study of all the ideas in the history of philosophy, but without being explicitly historical?

HEGEL: That's right. This is what I call "the development of the *concept*," in other words, the logical progression of the various ways in which people have *conceived* of the world.[4] But I should add that it is not just an account of the way in which *philosophers* have conceived of the world. They make a full-time business out of their conceptions, of course, but ordinary people, and poets and artists and saints and whole societies have their

4. Concept (*Begriff*); conceive (*begriffen*).

conceptions of the world, too, and it is just as important to take them into account.

BW: I very much agree Professor. And I now understand more clearly how the *Phenomenology* was supposed to be a study of the ways in which people have conceived of the world, in order to demonstrate that all their conceptions lead to the same conclusion—the Absolute, or the world conceived of as a unity.

HEGEL: Very good.

BW: Thank you. You said that the *Phenomenology* was supposed to be an introduction to the first volume of your "system," a book on logic and metaphysics?

HEGEL: Yes, I think I originally intended for it to be about one hundred pages long, at most.

BW: What happened?

HEGEL: You have it there on your table; the *Phenomenology* is almost five hundred pages long, and that was just supposed to be the "introduction."

BW: My, you did get carried away, didn't you?

HEGEL: I told you so. And to make matters worse, I started changing my conception of the book when I was about halfway through. The original idea was to present a series of conceptions of knowledge, beginning with the most naive conception—that the world is just "out there" and we know it only through experience—to the most sophisticated conception, that of "absolute knowing," which is the conclusion we've been talking about. At that point, when I had demonstrated that the world can be understood only in terms of the various ways in which we conceive of it . . .

BW: And that demonstration is the Absolute?

HEGEL: Yes.

BW: The word seems to keep shifting its meaning.

HEGEL: I know, but at that point I could begin the discussion of logic, which is simply the study of the various concepts through which we conceive the world.

BW: Why didn't you?

HEGEL: I never arrived there. On the way, it became increasingly clear to me that the various conceptions people have had of the world are much richer than the handful I had originally considered; and when I started to consider the details of history—the conception of life in Greek tragedy, the confusions of the French Revolution—it was virtually impossible to stop.

BW: How did you stop?

HEGEL: By screeching to a halt, essentially. I threw in a quick survey of all the religions in the world—from lecture notes I had prepared for my students—and then capped it off with "Absolute Knowing," rather like stuffing a cork in a wine barrel which is already overflowing.

BW: You don't sound entirely happy with your performance.

HEGEL: I'm not. I'm not *unhappy* with it, but the book is a reckless and ill-organized work. It served one essential purpose, namely, to establish the position from which my system makes sense, but it is something of a mess, and it has implications with which I now thoroughly disagree.

BW: What are those?

HEGEL: If you look at the book as a long series of different ways in which people have conceived of their world, culminating in a position, namely, "Absolute Knowing," which says that the Absolute is nothing but that series of ways of conceiving, the conclusion seems to be that there is no correct way in which to see the world. In fact, if ways of seeing determine the nature of the world, then there would be no single world but rather many worlds, one for each conception of it.

BW: And you don't accept that conclusion?

HEGEL: Of course not. Philosophy is concerned with eternal ideas; if I thought there weren't any answers, I wouldn't be in this business. I would do something practical such as sell shoes—a different size for every pair of feet.

BW: Would you be upset to hear that there are philosophers in the twentieth century who read you in the way you have just deplored?

HEGEL: I'm not surprised, but they're wrong; that's not what I believe at all.

BW: Now, you mean.

HEGEL: Now, of course. Who knows what I intended then? As I said, I got carried away in that book, almost possessed; that's why I don't do much with it anymore.

BW: Have you considered rewriting it?

HEGEL: Someday I might.[5]

BW: Let's take a brief break in our conversation, Professor. We'll be back in a moment, after station identification.

5. He was just starting to do so at the time of his death in 1831.

BW: Professor Hegel, this is an old question, but let me ask you again— why a "system" of philosophy? Why not just say what you believe and prove it?

HEGEL: Well, first of all, it is not what *I* believe that really counts, is it? What we have to find is what is *true,* and that means what everyone *must* believe, and that in turn means that a philosophy must be developed not only from my beliefs but from everyone's beliefs, no matter how different they may be. So philosophy must, first of all, be systematic in that sense; it can't just be an assortment of opinions and proofs on my part, but a systematic development of human thought as such. Second, nothing one believes is separable from anything else that one believes. Of course you can always pick out individual "facts," such as "Berlin is the capital of Prussia," but even that sentence makes sense only by being a part of an overall system of interconnected concepts and beliefs. What philosophy must do is to make that system, which in one sense is already implicit even in our every-day tasks and conversations, explicit.

BW: And Kant failed to do this, you believe, because he didn't show the connections between knowledge and free action?

HEGEL: Right; it is absurd to suggest that what one knows about the world, in a scientific theory, for example, has nothing to do with what one does or has to do as a matter of practical necessity; and it is equally absurd to think that those scientific theories one believes in have nothing to do with what you might call one's more "religious" views, and one's sense of beauty, morals, metaphors, taste in vegetables—in short, with everything.

BW: But it was Kant who wanted to reconcile knowledge and religion, morality, art and so on.

HEGEL: Yes. Unfortunately, however, he separated them rather than brought them together.

BW: Do you think cause-and-effect determinism and free action are compatible?

HEGEL: No, but I reject the universality of cause–and–effect determinism. My view of scientific knowledge is much more akin to Leibniz and Aristotle than to Newton; I think understanding nature is far more like understanding a living organism than understanding the workings of a watch.

BW: Isn't that what Schelling used to argue too?

HEGEL: Yes it is, in a sense, except that he never really worked it out. What would it be like to see world-spirit as a living, growing organism rather than as an all-encompassing lump of matter?

BW: And that picture is what you have created?

HEGEL: Yes, my *Phenomenology* is essentially a portrait of world-spirit or *Geist* growing up. It is the same portrait one finds in Aristotle's metaphysics, more or less—the cosmos becoming self-conscious, "thought thinking itself." And that of course, is where my *Logic* begins.

BW: With "thought thinking itself"; what does that mean?

HEGEL: Essentially, thinking about thinking, which is what philosophers do all the time.

BW: And the rest of the "system"?

HEGEL: It is a synthesis of logic, and a philosophy of nature—demonstrating that nature, too, must be understood as a systematic development of forms, *living* forms . . .

BW: Even, say, mechanics or the law of gravity?

HEGEL: Yes, and electricity and magnetism; all such phenomena can be comprehended only in the perspective of their role in a living universe. And then, finally, the philosophy of spirit, which shows how the workings of our individual minds and our social institutions also follow the same development of conceptual forms. As I said, you can't really understand any facet of human experience without understanding the others, as well.

BW: This "development" that you keep mentioning—I assume that is what is called your "*dialectic*."

HEGEL: Yes, dialectic is essentially a development of different forms, whether they are forms of thinking, forms of nature or forms of government.

BW: Is dialectic essentially history then?

HEGEL: No, not necessarily. Earlier we talked about the relation between various ideas in philosophy and the history of philosophy, and the fact that they more or less manifest the same logical sequence. But this sequence does not have to be displayed historically. Indeed, in some disciplines—for example, mathematics—a historical chronology of theorems would be pretty much beside the point. The moves would all be there, but in a much too contingent and circumstantial manner. It is the logic connecting them that interests us.

BW: Why do you need a dialectic at all? Why couldn't you just present these various ideas, or forms, in a single systematic manner?

HEGEL: Because the systematic manner *is* the way in which one form develops into another when you examine them. Concepts and such don't have their independent existence and interconnections apart from being thought about, whether consciously and reflectively, as in philosophy, or worked through in a practical manner, as people do, for example, when they are struggling to establish an adequate form of government, as in the French Revolution and its complex aftermath.

BW: I see. What would be an example of a dialectical movement?

HEGEL: Here is a simple one: Suppose a philosopher says that there is only one thing in the world, which we can call "Being." It sounds right, even obvious: everything that is, is Being. But when you push that view, what becomes evident is that having a conception of Being already presupposes a conception of what it would be for any given thing, and perhaps even everything, *not* to be. So one cannot have a conception of "Being" without a conception of "Not-being" as well.

BW: I see.

HEGEL: And once you understand that you can't conceive of "Being" without "Not-being" too, the question becomes, how do those two concepts tie together?

BW: As opposites? "Thesis and antithesis?"

HEGEL: No, that language won't help at all. We have a conception of "Being" and "Not-being" together because we have a conception of how a thing comes to be, how it is born, how it develops, how it changes, dies or disappears. In other words, the new concept is "Becoming."

BW: In your whole philosophy, I see that the idea of change and growth keeps coming up at every crucial point. Is that right?

HEGEL: Definitely. That is what "dialectic" is all about— *change.* This is perhaps my biggest argument against Kant. Do you remember fifteen years ago, when you asked us what we thought Kant's most important contribution was? I said, the discovery of "dialectic." But Kant didn't know what to do with it; he thought he had discovered merely the limits of reason, namely, that pure reason seems to prove contradictory theses. What he should have realized was that he had proven that our conceptions of the world are not fixed, as he had argued in his first *Critique,* but flexible. We can look at the world in different ways and the world, in turn, becomes very different for us.

BW: So what you reject is Kant's view that the categories of understanding are fixed and necessary, or "a priori" as he would say?

HEGEL: Yes; I reject both the mechanical bias of his categories and the rigid form in which he presented them. He never thought about how concepts change at all; in fact, he just picked up his list of categories from the local psychologists, as if they were any authority on human understanding.

BW: Whereas it is changes in concepts that rule your philosophy, or dialectic?

HEGEL: Yes, or dialectic.

BW: Doesn't dialectic essentially means conflict, two positions warring against each other until some resolution, or synthesis, comes along?

HEGEL: That whole "thesis–antithesis–synthesis" triad is too wooden and inflexible to fit all the different movements of concepts. Of course you can cram a movement into that form if you try hard enough, but sometimes the dialectic proceeds on the basis of conflict and opposition, whereas at other times the forms cooperate and improve on one another. There isn't any fixed rule, any more than there are any particular fixed concepts. "Dialectic" essentially means "conversation," and a conversation can progress in any number of ways. But that doesn't make it "illogical" either.

BW: I see. What is the purpose of your dialectic, if that is a fair question?

HEGEL: Oh, it is a very fair question. Indeed, the whole point of dialectic, in every field of human endeavor, is to realize some purpose toward which that whole endeavor is aimed.

BW: At one point didn't you say that the ultimate purpose is always *truth?*

HEGEL: Yes, but "truth" in general is nothing but the goal; the "truth" of art is beauty, the "truth" of morality is right action, the "truth" of science is the best explanation, and so on, just as a "true friend" is the ideal friend and "true aim" is aim that hits the mark.

BW: And dialectic is the realization of this "truth," in each case?

HEGEL: Yes, the dialectic of the book I am just completing, which will be called *The Philosophy of Right,* is a study in the various forms of social order, for the purpose of demonstrating the implicit ideals in all of them and to show what single form of government is the best realization of these ideals.

BW: And which government is that?

HEGEL: Ours, of course! The real is rational, after all, or as Alexander Pope put it, "Whatever is, is right."

BW: That's convenient.

HEGEL: What else can one do? What's the point of wishing for something else? The point of philosophy is to help us appreciate what we have. And I do the same for religion, for art—for any human endeavor.

BW: I see; do you compare different endeavors, say, religion, art, philosophy and science, to see which of their goals and ideals is the best?

HEGEL: Indeed I do. That is what I do in the *Phenomenology* and also in my *Philosophy of Spirit*.

BW: Which one wins?

HEGEL: [*chortles*] Philosophy wins, of course!

BW: Therefore we may say that philosophy is the best, the "highest" human activity, the one that realizes the ideals of all others?

HEGEL: Yes, but not without them too, of course.

BW: Have you always believed that?

HEGEL: Goodness, no. As a youth I used to think that morality was the highest human endeavor, which is why I was so attracted to Fichte. When I was close to Schelling in Jena I tended to agree with him that religion was the highest endeavor, although I always disagreed with him about the importance of art.

BW: You don't think that art is important?

HEGEL: I don't think it is *most* important. He did.

BW: In that light, let me ask you if you can give a simple answer to the following question: what is the purpose of your own philosophy? What is the "highest" human endeavor, in your opinion?

HEGEL: Philosophy, in a phrase, is our attempt *to make sense of the world*.

BW: Does it need making sense of?

HEGEL: How can you even ask? In childhood, perhaps, the meaningfulness of life was given to us, along with our baby food and our language. But now, particularly during the tumultuous years of the last several decades, what is "given" to us has simply been confusion. The world is a mass of contradictions; our society is a sickly reflection of inefficient governments and citizens who have no sense of participation in their communities or their state. History is a slaughterbench on which the fortunes and happiness of whole nations have been sacrificed. The business of philosophy is to make sense of this awesome inheritance, to demonstrate that life does indeed have a meaning.

BW: And could you describe that meaning?

HEGEL: Yes, in a word: "Spirit." The meaning of life is to be found in our painful and slow recognition that we are all one people, one *humanity,* as Kant used to say, and in the fact that it is, after thousands of years of struggle, a wholly human world, the world of human spirit.

BW: Was it worth it?

HEGEL: It would be irrational to believe otherwise; it's all we have.

BW: This "spirit" you talk about is, I assume, the same character in both your *Phenomenology of Spirit* and your *Philosophy of Spirit*; can you tell us what exactly it is?

HEGEL: It's everything, really. But more precisely, it is the self-consciousness of the world, which manifests itself through human consciousness.

BW: Doesn't "spirit" mean God? It sounds as if it means God.

HEGEL: Yes, it does, and it doesn't. I do believe in God, if that's what you mean. But it is an *immanent* God—in the theological jargon, a God that is "in us," in fact, *is* us.

BW: Then spirit—or God—is nothing more than human beings?

HEGEL: Again, yes and no. There is no God "up there," if that's what it would be for Him to be "something more" than human. But God is not identical to any particular human being either, or to any group of human beings. God is all of us, and our whole world.

BW: Isn't that called "pantheism"?

HEGEL: No, pantheism is a vulgar materialist philosophy that identifies God with mere matter.[6] Hindus, for instance, think God is in their cows. I use the word "spirit" for a reason, to emphasize the "spiritual" nature of God. But, of course, He's substance too.

BW: It sounds the same to me, with a slight shift of emphasis.

HEGEL: [*with a smile*] A slight shift of emphasis, perhaps, but careers and even the truth may depend on such slight shifts of emphasis.

BW: You often write as if God—or spirit—is something not only within us but also something which uses us for its own purposes. For example, I have heard that you sometimes use the phrase "the cunning of reason," as if reason, or spirit, were some force manipulating individuals for its purpose.

6. See footnote 6, p. 53.

HEGEL: Another shift of emphasis, although not so slight. It is a common Germanic manner of thinking; for example, Goethe always talks of his genius as a "daemon" inside of him, which possesses him and leads him to wherever it wants. Now, on the one hand, this is obviously nonsense; his genius *is he himself*. But the experience certainly has this other aspect too; it is as if the voice of the German spirit were speaking through him, an experience anyone who has ever been a spokesman for anything will recognize. So too, one could look at language "speaking through" a person as well as the person speaking the language. In a like manner, "spirit" is the spirit of humanity, the whole history of human experience, speaking through each one of us.

BW: And in particular through you philosophers?

HEGEL: Yes. It used to speak through priests and oracles but now it speaks through philosophers. Of course, the human spirit speaks through everyone else as well, just not so explicitly.

BW: You think spirit manifests itself in every human activity then?

HEGEL: Yes, a craftsman making a bowl, a teacher conveying the wisdom of a culture, a chemist trying to develop a new soap, all of them are expressions of the human spirit struggling to recognize itself as such.

BW: You make it sound as if self-recognition is everything.

HEGEL: If you examine yourself, I think you will find that your self-conception, your sense of identity and esteem, is far more important and pervasive than you believe, even more important than the urge to survive.

BW: It's true, most people would rather die than be totally humiliated, and those who choose otherwise soon *wish* they were dead. In some primitive tribes, being exiled is considered worse than being killed.

HEGEL: Yes. Belonging is everything. Aristotle saw it twenty-five hundred years ago, when he said that "man is a social animal." It is one of the peculiarities of modern society that we think that the absolute element of human life is the *individual*. But the individual has significance only as a member of a particular society, a particular culture, and, ultimately, by being human and recognizing the same humanity in all of us.

BW: Which is more important, being human or being a member of a particular society?

HEGEL: Ah, that is the most difficult question. The Enlightenment, of course, including Kant, thought that the only important identity was the recognition of oneself and everyone else as human, as part of humanity. Local customs and cultural differences didn't count, except as matters of provincial prejudice and as curiosities. Then there was the anti-Enlightenment attack by people such as Johann Herder, who insisted that what was most important was culture, particular peoples, the *Volk*. For him and others like him, "humanity" was just an abstraction. That is why the romantics, as you probably know, made so much of our "Gothic" ancestry, trying to dig up a mythological historical past to give us Germans a cultural identity.

BW: Because you have no real political identity?

HEGEL: Right. Our identity has been our language, and now our poetry and philosophy.

BW: That is why poetry and philosophy are so important here, and why poets and philosophers—you and Goethe, for example—are the national heroes.

HEGEL: Right again. But to answer your question, I think it is impossible to choose between cultural identity and human identity; they require one another. Spirit is the absolute, but it exists only in its various distinct cultural forms; you can't have just "humanity." Humanity is the unified whole of all of the different cultures of the world, and the differences count just as much as the identity.

BW: But what doesn't count for you, I take it, is the individual?

HEGEL: No, the individual doesn't count, that is, as an individual. He or she counts as part of a larger identity, as part of a family, or a community, or a culture, and, of course, spirit as such. Try to identify yourself "as an individual," without immediately appealing to social categories, comparisons with others or, in desperation, by "just being a human being."

BW: During the Napoleonic battles when you formulated this notion, I can imagine you visualizing a field of hundreds of thousands of soldiers, distinguished only by the colors of their uniforms. In that perspective, it must indeed be humbling to realize how little the individual counts, except as a tiny piece of these larger forces.

HEGEL: Yes, something like that experience surely lies behind my perspective.

BW: Don't you agree, however, that some viewers may be put off by your philosophy because it does make so little of the individual?

HEGEL: But the point is that your modern fetish of the individual is fraudulent. In the *Phenomenology,* for instance, I go through a series of arguments to show how vain and ultimately empty our conceptions of individual pleasure, individual power, individual virtue, individual happiness, inevitably turn out to be.

BW: Do you deny the possibility of individual pleasure, power, virtue, and happiness?

HEGEL: No, of course not. What I am saying is that these can only be realized within the context of a larger social picture.

BW: Does this mean that the values themselves—what gives us pleasure or power, what counts as virtue or happiness—are given to us by society, too?

HEGEL: Yes and no. Yes, we learn these things in a particular culture, of course, but please don't make it sound as if societies are simply "given," just "there." We determine the nature of our society, for example, every time we obey, or refuse to obey, the law. Societies too are subject to change, and they do change, as we are forced to reflect on ourselves and resolve the internal tensions and shortcomings of any particular social arrangement.

BW: But I would think virtue, the basic laws of morality, would exist apart from *any* particular culture. Don't you agree that a person can rightly condemn his or her entire society for its immoral conduct or unjust laws?

HEGEL: Of course, but from what standpoint? You see, this idea of morality as a set of absolute rules, or "categorical imperatives" as Kant called them, embodies a great deal of confusion. It is true that we formulate moral principles and apply them even to our society as a whole, but what Kant falsely concludes from this is that the principles are primary, and that morality is simply a matter of principle, nothing else.

BW: And it isn't?

HEGEL: No, of course not. And it couldn't be even if one *wanted* to formulate a morality based on rules alone. Abstract principles have to be applied, but how? One needs a rule for the application of the rule. And does that mean you need another rule to tell you how to apply the rule? And so, *ad infinitum.*

BW: I agree that there is a problem in applying abstract moral rules, but don't you agree, nevertheless, that morality consists of rules?

HEGEL: No. Of course, as I said, one can always formulate rules, but that is not how we learn morality, that is not the content of our morality, and that is not how we justify our morality. As children, we learn that certain things should or shouldn't be done. We grow up doing or not doing those things, and we justify our doing or not doing them, ultimately, because "this must be done" or "these things are not done."

BW: But doesn't that mean that moral principles can't be justified, that they are whatever a society decides they should be?

HEGEL: But that *is* justification, if indeed those rules are generally accepted and do indeed allow the society to function as a coherent unity. What more could one possibly want? And in any case, that is all you can get.

BW: What about Kant's claim that categorical imperatives— moral laws—are *logical* necessities, that breaking them brings about logical contradictions?

HEGEL: You mean, if the generalization of your action brings about logical contradictions; but, first of all, it is virtually never the case that everyone, in fact, will do what you are considering doing. And second, even if they did, what would that prove? For example: suppose everyone were to take anything he or she wanted—*steal,* in other words—whenever it suited that person. Now the Kantian argument is that this would lead to a contradiction, because it would then no longer make any sense to say "this is mine," for property would be only a matter of possession and not a matter of right, and therefore there could be no such act as "stealing." But there are some socialists here in Berlin who would say, "very good; that's just what we should do, abolish private property." So what does the so-called "contradiction" prove, that one should not steal? Or, if you are a socialist, that one should?

BW: But what justifies a culture in having certain moral laws, or, if not laws, then . . .

HEGEL: Practices, you might say, or *customs.* In fact, in many of my writings I distinguish my view from Kant's by distinguishing his concept of morality (*moralität*) from my notion of *Sittlichkeit* (where *"Sitte"* simply means "custom" or "mores"). What justifies a practice or a custom or a law is that it works. One can criticize a society, even one's own society, by showing that the practice doesn't work, or it is inconsistent, or that people are saying one thing and doing something quite different.

BW: In other words, you appeal to the practice itself, and not some overriding moral law.

HEGEL: Yes, what good is it if I go up to a cannibal chieftan and say, "My dear chief, it is immoral to eat one's prisoners"? But what I can do is to show him that his own practice is somehow unworkable, or that there is no justification for it *in his own terms.*

BW: What would be an example of an unworkable practice, or a contradition within a morality? Let's *not* talk about cannibalism.

HEGEL: Well, my favorite example is the Greek tragedy *Antigone,* which marks the transition from tribal society to what you might call civil society with an abstract set of laws and so on. You know the story: Antigone is torn between her family duty to bury her dead brother, and her civic duty to obey Creon, who has forbidden it. There was a point at which Greek society incorporated both family loyalties and civil duties, without giving either clear priority; the Antigone story shows what is wrong with that kind of community.

BW: How does the contradiction get resolved?

HEGEL: For Antigone and Creon, it doesn't. But what happens in both history and in logic is that civil society gains priority, so that in later Greek and Roman mythology, for example, you often find heroes sacrificing their families to the community demands.

BW: And is that good? I mean, doesn't that lead to increasingly impersonal institutions and states, like our modern bureaucracies?

HEGEL: Bureaucracies may be impersonal—they are designed to be impersonal—but they need not be detached from the interests of the community. Indeed, that is the problem for us now, to develop some modern sense of *Sittlichkeit,* a sense of community and shared values. Our societies are too much based on abstract laws and the threat of punishment to keep people in line, rather than their own sense of participation and cultural identity.

BW: Was it ever any different, Professor?

HEGEL: Of course. It was different in Greece, for example. The Greek city-state, or *polis,* gave every citizen a sense of participation, so that the interests and virtues of the individual were identical to the interests and virtues of the *polis.* One did not have to be forced to be a good citizen; to be a good citizen was the same as realizing one's own potential as a person.

BW: What happened?

HEGEL: Well, societies grew much larger, for one thing. That small community spirit became impossible to maintain. Christianity came along, with its doctrines of unworldliness and the rejection of society, and its conception of the individual in opposition to society. In fact, modern political theory is wholly caught up in this problem of how the individual can be brought to accept the legitimate demands of society. The Greeks would not have understood that question, for there was no individual who was not already part of society. But today our best theorists—Jean-

Jacques Rousseau, John Locke, Thomas Hobbes—believe that the origins of society and the justification of society's demands are based on an implicit agreement, a *social* contract, in which all individuals agree to give up certain freedoms in exchange for the benefits of society.

BW: And you don't believe in such a "social contract"?

HEGEL: I think it is nonsense; there are no individuals prior to society. An individual is what his society makes him. The problem is not to give legitimacy to society and the state but to reintegrate the citizen and his sense of participation in society.

BW: This raises a very difficult topic, Professor Hegel. You wouldn't know this but your philosophy has been used in our century as a justification for some cruel and despotic societies. In particular, your notion of participation in society and your insistence on the relative unimportance of the individual has been used to justify governments that deny all freedoms to their citizens except for what they call "the freedom to obey." Now surely this isn't what you had in mind?

HEGEL: I'm horrified by what you say but let me be very clear about what I mean by "freedom." I do indeed say that freedom is to be found only in one's participation in the society as a whole, that freedom isn't possible for an isolated individual. But this doesn't mean "freedom to obey," in the sense I think you are using it. That is tyranny, and as you know, my whole philosophy is a defense of freedom. I reject the social contract, but I have always accepted the core of liberal political philosophy: the rights of individuals *within* the society, religious tolerance and freedom of speech, the importance of a constitutional representational government . . .

BW: You still believe in monarchy, however.

HEGEL: Yes, of course; the state needs a figurehead, a personal representation of its character, but I believe in a *constitutional* monarchy, in which the people are represented and the monarch is limited by law.

BW: I see, but freedom . . .

HEGEL: "Freedom." Yes, but you have to understand the context in which we are working. I see our primary problem not only as interference in the lives of citizens by the government but as an absence of any worthy state with which citizens can proudly identify themselves—a lack of *Sittlichkeit* and community. And it is in that light that I emphasize what we sometimes call "positive freedom," that is, the freedom to participate, to identify with and to realize one's potential within society.

BW: That sounds like your description of the Greek *polis.*

HEGEL: Of course; that has always been my ideal. In fact, I remember writing as a youth, "a community of men tied together by bonds of common brotherhood—can anyone imagine anything happier than that?" I still believe that, even if the Greeks are no longer a model for us. And, again, that is what my philosophy attempts to bring about.

BW: Professor Hegel, thank you very much for your time and for a most enjoyable discussion.

HEGEL: I enjoyed it myself, and I hope the twentieth century is not too bad for you. It is impossible for us to predict the consequences of our actions, you know. The future seems so far away. The twentieth century—I can't even imagine it. Why I can barely think about the next decade with any sense of confidence; things change so.

BW: And so they must, according to your own philosophy. [*to camera*] From Berlin, this is Barbara Wahrheit. We've just had the pleasure of talking with Professor G. W. F. Hegel, the reigning philosopher—king of the not so roaring 1820s. Please stay tuned for the evening news. Good night.

A Viewer's Response: ARTHUR SCHOPENHAUER

[*DBS television studio in Berlin. Camera takes close-up of earnest-looking announcer Sander J. Schmidt, who begins to speak*]

SJS: Good evening! I'm Sander J. Schmidt, Program Director of DBS, who welcomes you to "VIEWER'S RESPONSE," a weekly showcase featuring comment from our viewers in response to our programming. Of course, the opinions presented are those of the writer and not necessarily those of the network or the local sponsors. Our first letter tonight comes to us from a Herr Arthur Schopenhauer, Berlin, Prussia, and is dated January 21, 1820. It is quite an impassioned commentary which I think you will find most provocative and which we present uncensored. [*reads letter*]

My Dear DBS:

It was with profound disgust that I watched the last two shows of your thirty-year series on "German Idealism." Unfortunately, as I was only two years old at the time, I missed the first program, which may well have been the only one worth watching. I agree that Immanuel Kant is the greatest philosopher of our era, indeed, of any era; but the fact that you had the poor taste to memorialize him with that bunch of frauds and charlatans who call themselves "German Idealists" discredits you in the eyes of all who take philosophy seriously and who see the Kantian philosophy in particular as the highest achievement of the human will. And your stupidity and credulity—not to mention the possibility of your own vulgar ambitions in Berlin—in presenting that mumbleheaded academic ass Hegel as a rival of the great Kant make me actually embarrassed to be part of the same species—philosophers, that is, not academic asses.

If you want to know what German Idealism is, following the great Kant, I will tell you. It is not "Spirit" and all that mumbojumbo about the Absolute. It is r ot that stuffy patriot Fichte nor that *idiot savant* Schelling, much less that metaphysical clown Hegel. It is, in accordance with Kant's own philosophy, a two-fold development of the world as a series of *representations,* constructed by the finite mind of man, and the true thing-in-itself, *the infinite will,* which manifests itself in all of us, and drives us on and on and on, but to no purpose whatsoever. Hegel and his cronies have spent their entire muddled and unjustly rewarded careers trying to do the impossible—to prove that there is a purpose to it all. But there is no purpose; there is just *will.* And all that philosophy can do is to make us appreciate that fact, to console us in our vanity, to free us from those violent passions that render us bereft without leading anywhere.

What Kant saw so clearly, and Hegel and his cronies deny, is that there is a difference between what *is* and what can be rationally *known.* What we know, we know by the application of the concepts of our understanding to the sensations caused in the body, interpreted by way of reason. But this means that all knowledge is conditioned, as Kant insisted, not "absolute" as Hegel says. There may be sufficient reasons for our experiences and ideas being as they are, but that does not mean that the phenomenal world is not an illusion of reality, rather than reality itself. Reality indeed lies behind what the Oriental mystics call the "veil of Maya," not perceived or known by us. And much of what we call "reality"—space, time and causality, for example—are illusions too, created by our understanding and not in the things–themselves.

How do we know the things-in-themselves, you ask. Well, surely not by way of reason, as "the professors of philosophy" have argued, and not through that philosophical fog called "dialectic," either. We know the thing-in-itself by identifying with it, not through the senses or through space and time or through causal relationships but by *being* it, as *Will.* Kant saw this, except that he underestimated his own discovery, and he leaped too quickly to the conclusion that this Will was inherently rational, which it is not. But it is Will that brings about all of our thoughts as well as our actions, both voluntary and involuntary, conscious or unconscious. It is Will that one sees throughout Nature too, as Will to Life, in every living thing and even in what we call nonliving things too. Gravitation is the manifestation of Will just as much as the growth of plants. Try to kill an insect, and you will see the Will at work; it struggles even after death, each part of its body making one last movement, as if to assert itself once more. And we too, both in those acts we call "free " and those for which we do not take responsibility at all, express the One Infinite Will in our every breath, our every movement, our every thought and gesture.

But the great Kant erred, I'm afraid, when he described Will in the narrowest terms of morality, in terms of those few actions where our own principles and ends are in evidence. There are such actions, of course, but even they are the manifestation of a Will that is blind and without purpose. This is Hegel's mistake, too; he believes that what he calls "Reason" determines the goal and direction of life. There is the Will to Life, but to what end? Look at those insects who live their entire lives so that one night only they can take to the skies and mate—and die. And why? So that they can have offspring who can do the same thing next year, and so on, forever. Think of a common mole, burrowing through the ground, eating bugs to keep alive, living its entire life in darkness, and you have a far more accurate view of human life than you will find in Hegel's epic descriptions. We too live, struggle to keep alive, reproduce and die in darkness. Why? There is no answer. There is no goal. There is no purpose to it all. There is no good in life; there is just life itself. Of course, one can still try to live it to the fullest, and I intend to do so—but without the illusion of purpose. Without the vanity that life leads to something. Without the pretention that human life is any different from life in general, an expression of an irrational Will whose only end is its own continued existence.

And yet Hegel, that pied piper, promises his students something more, some absolute purpose and divine realization of themselves—and so they flock to his courses. I know, I taught with him, or rather against him, in Berlin, and do you know that students just poured into his incomprehensible, hypocritical lectures. *And ignored mine!* And so they have all come to think of Hegel as the logical successor to Kant, and your nitwit network has come to believe them too. But Hegel is not the successor to Kant; *I am. Arthur Schopenhauer.*

The key to Kant is the Will as the thing-in-itself, that infinite force driving itself through us, and I alone have shown that this indeed is the true philosophy, assuming that my readers already know their Kant, of course. The world is an illusion, and it is by seeing through the illusion to the meaninglessness of it all that life can be made, let's say, tolerable. Some say I'm a pessimist; I guess that I am. But if it is pessimistic to see through the follies of the world and expose as frauds one's fellow philosophers, then I'm proud to be a pessimist. One of my few students even had the audacity, a few weeks ago, to ask me if my conception of infinite Will was not pretty much the same as Hegel's conception of "Spirit." Can you imagine? I flunked him, of course, after beating him with my walking stick and throwing him out of my office on his ears. I have a mind to do the same with the executives of your network too. They deserve a good hiding, if for nothing else, to teach them something about what the world is really like.

"German Idealism" —the nerve, the gall, the stupidity! If you want to do a really interesting program on philosophy and give a genuine tribute to the genius of Kant, invite *me* for an interview. But hurry, I intend to be very famous soon. My book, by the way, published just last year—althought the idiots in your book-review program ignored it completely—is called THE WORLD AS WILL AND REPRESENTATION. And I am,

Cordially,

Arthur Schopenhauer,
the only true
    "German idealist"

A BRIEF BIBLIOGRAPHY

I. Kant

Basic Works (in English translation):

The Critique of Judgment. Translated by J. C. Meredith. Oxford, 1952.

The Critique of Practical Reason. Translated by L. W. Beck. New York, 1956.

The Critique of Pure Reason. Translated by N. Kemp Smith. New York, 1966.

Grounding (*Foundations*) *for the Metaphysics of Morals.* Translated by J. W. Ellington. Indianapolis, 1981.

Idea of a Universal History. Translated by W. Hastie in *Theories of History.* Edited by P. Gardiner. New York, 1958.

Lectures on Ethics. Translated by L. Infield. Indianapolis, 1981.

The Metaphysical Principles of Virtue. Translated by M. J. Gregor. New York, 1949.

Metaphysics of Morals, Part I; *Metaphysical Elements of Justice,* Part II. Translated by J. Ladd. Indianapolis, 1956.

Perpetual Peace. Translated by L. W. Beck. New York, 1939.

Philosophical Correspondence, 1759–99. Translated and edited by A. Zweig. Chicago, 1967.

A Prolegomena to Any Future Metaphysics. Revised by J. W. Ellington from Carus (1902). Indianapolis, 1977.

Religion Within the Limits of Reason Alone. Translated by T. M. Green. New York, 1960.

Books about Kant's Philosophy:

Good works about Kant's philosophy are also plentiful; particularly recommended are the following:

Beck, L. W. *Commentary on Kant's Critique of Practical Reason.* Chicago, 1962.

Bennett, J. *Kant's Analytic.* Cambridge, 1966.

Heidegger, M. *Kant and the Problem of Metaphysics.* Translated by J. Churchill. Bloomington, Ind., 1962.

Jones, W. T. *Morality and Freedom in Kant.* London, 1940.

Korner, S. *Kant.* Baltimore, 1967.

Paton, H. J. *The Categorical Imperative.* Chicago, 1948.

Ross, Sir W. D. *Kant's Ethical Theory.* Oxford, 1954.

Sellars, W. *Science and Metaphysics.* London. 1968.

Smith, Norman K. *Commentary on Kant's Critique of Pure Reason.* London, 1958.

Strawson, P. F. *The Bounds of Sense.* London, 1966.

Weldon, *Introduction to Kant's Critique for Pure Reason,* 1958.

Wolff, R. P. *Kant's Theory of Mental Activity.* Cambridge, Mass., 1965.

Wolff, R. P., ed. *Kant: A Collection of Critical Essays.* Garden City, N.Y., 1967.

II. **Fichte,** *et al.* (selected works in English translation):

Fichte, G. *Science of Knowledge.* Translated by Heath and Lachs. New York, 1970.

————. *The Vocation of Man.* Translated by Smith. Indianapolis, Bobbs-Merrill, 1956.

Schelling, F. *System of Transcendental Philosophy.* Translated by F. Schelling. Chicago, 1936.

Schelling, F. *On Human Freedom.* Translated by J. Guttman. Chicago, 1936.

on Fichte, Schelling, Reinhold, *see*

Hegel, G.W.F. *The Difference Between Fichte's and Schelling's System of Philosophy.* Translated by Harris and Cerf. Albany, 1977. Contains an excellent long introduction by the translators.

for a good picture of romanticism in general, *see*

Abrams, M. H. *Natural and Supernatural.* Norton, 1971. (especially Chapters 3 and 4)

III. **Hegel** (in English translation):

Early Theological Writings. Nos. III and IV. Translated by Knox. New York, 1961.

The Phenomenology of Spirit. Translated by A. V. Miller. Oxford, 1977.

The Philosophy of Right. Translated by Knox. Oxford, 1967.

The Science of Logic. 2 vols. Translated by W. H. Johnston and L. G. Struthers. London, 1929.

"Lesser' Logic." Translated by W. Wallace in *Encyclopedia.* Part I. Oxford, 1874.

"Hegel's Philosophy of Mind." Translated by W. Wallace. In *Encyclopedia.* Part III. Oxford, 1894.

Hegel's Philosophy of Nature. Translated by A. V. Miller, J. N. Findlay. *Encyclopedia.* Part II. New York, 1970.

Hegel's famous *Lectures* are edited together from students' notes and lecture notes, and so are less dependable than the above works. Most are available only in expensive editions, but they are beginning to appear in paperback selections:

Lectures on Philosophy of History. Translated by J. Sibree. New York, 1956. "Introduction" to the *Lectures.* Translated by R. S. Hartman in *Reason in History.* New York, 1953.

Philosophy of Fine Art. Translated by F. Osmaston. London, 1920.

On the Philosophy of Religion, 3 vols. Translated by Spiers and Sanderson. London, 1895.

On the History of Philosophy. Translated by E. Haldane and F. Simson. London, 1892–1896.

Selections from these last three are now available in paperback:

Hegel on Art, Religion, and Philosophy. Edited by J. Glen Gray. New York, 1970.

Many of Hegel's letters are available in W. Kaufmann's *Hegel: A Reinterpretation* (New York, 1965), which also contains a translation of the "Preface" to the *Phenomenology.*

Books about Hegel's Philosophy. There are no truly introductory books on Hegel's philosophy, but for the more advanced philosophy student, some of the following may prove helpful:

J. N. Findlay. *The Philosophy of Hegel.* New York, 1964.

W. Kaufmann. *Hegel: A Reinterpretation.* New York, 1966.

M. Marcuse. *Reason and Revolution.* Boston, 1960.

R. Plant. *Hegel.* London, 1978.

I. Soll. *An Introduction to Hegel's Metaphysics.* Chicago, 1969.

R. Solomon. *In the Spirit of Hegel.* New York, forthcoming.

C. Taylor. *Hegel.* Cambridge, 1969.

C. Taylor. *Hegel and Modern Society.* Cambridge, 1979.

IV. On Schopenhauer:

Schopenhauer's primary work is *The World as Will and Representation,* translated by E. F. J. Payne. Colorado, 1958. Shorter, more accessible works are:

The Will to Live. Ed. by R. Taylor. New York, 1962.

Selected Essays. Ed. by T. B. Saunders. London, 1951.

Essay on the Freedom of the Will. Translated by K. Kolenda. New York, 1960.

A good secondary reading is P. Gardiner, *Schopenhauer.* London, 1963.